Columbia Country Records Discography 1924-1932

Compiled By
Christian Scott

Every effort has been made by the author and publisher of this book to provide accurate information on the subject of this book. Even though the information in this book has been carefully checked and researched, the author and publisher disclaim any responsibility for errors in the book.

No portion of this publication may be reproduced in any form or by any means, electronic or mechanical, including recording, photocopying or by any information storage or retrieval system, without written permission from the author and publisher.

This book is dedicated to my wife Eileen, my best friend, the love of my life, a wonderful woman with a beautiful soul and a giving heart.

Columbia Country Records Discography 1924 - 1932

Copyright 2010 R. Lees

All Rights Reserved.

All Pictures and Names Used Remain "Trademark" and "Copyright" of Their Respective Rights Holders.

ISBN-13: 978-1456487416

ISBN-10: 1456487418

Acknowledgements

I would like to express my appreciation to all the people who contributed their time, assistance, research, knowledge and yes their corrections as well throughout the process of creating this reference guide. Their assistance has been indispensable.

Table of Contents

Acknowledgments……………………………………………...1

About the Book……………….…………………………...…3

Format (How To Use This Book)……..……………………4

Discography……………………………………………….…5

Bibliography………………………………………………..92

Index of Artists……………………………………………93

Acknowledgements

I would like to express my appreciation to all the people who contributed their time, assistance, research, knowledge and yes their corrections as well throughout the process of creating this reference guide. Their assistance has been indispensable.

Table of Contents

Acknowledgments……………………………………………..…1

About the Book………………….………………………...…3

Format (How To Use This Book)……..………………………..4

Discography………………………………………………….5

Bibliography……………………………………………..…92

Index of Artists……………………………………………93

About the Book

This book is designed to be a reference guide for the Columbia 15000-D Hillbilly / Country Series records (also known as the Columbia Old Familiar Tunes Series) which were produced from 1924 – 1932.

782 different records were issued in the 8 year run of this series, starting with number 15000-D and ending with 15782-D.

This book is organized in alphabetical order by artist and includes:

> Full Artist(s) name and pseudonyms they recorded under for the Columbia 15000-D series
>
> Cross referencing of artists / pseudonyms and who they recorded with on the Columbia 15000-D series
>
> Full title details
>
> Dates and Matrix numbers

Many references have been consulted in order to complete this discography. However, I am sure that errors and omissions are present and I hope that they will be brought to my attention you can send an e-mail to **recordguides@gmail.com.**

Format Of This Book (How To Use)

This book is formatted similar to a discography. The artist(s) will be listed in all **Bold** caps. The issue number will be listed below the name and to the left. If a pseudonym is used or if additional artist details are required to be shown they will be next to the issue number in **Bold** parentheses. The date (if the same for both recordings) will be printed to the right of the issue number and or after the additional details shown in parentheses. If additional room is required for the date it will be listed on the line below the issue number and printed on the right side. If there are two different dates to be shown they will be listed after the matrix numbers. Song titles will be listed in full below the issue number and matrix numbers (when known) will be listed to the right of the song titles.

See Examples Below:

CANOVA FAMILY
15630-D (as by Three Georgia Crackers)
....(Dec 18, 1930)
I've Been Hoodooed............................mx 151159-3
Whoa, Buck, Whoa..............................mx 151165-2

15653-D (as by Three Georgia Crackers)
Poor Little Thing Cried Mammy
.............................mx 151160-2 / Dec 18, 1930
Hannah, My Love................mx 151168-2 / Dec 19, 1930

GREEN B. ADAIR

15166-D..(Mar 26, 1927)
Talkin' About My Gal............................mx 143777-2
A Trip To The City................................mx 143778-1

15316-D..(Nov 9, 1927)
Lucy Wants Insurance...........................mx 145190-2
Malinda Gets Married............................mx 145191-3

AKINS BIRMINGHAM BOYS

15348-D..(Oct 31, 1928)
I Walked And Walked...........................mx 147356-2
There Ain't No Flies On Auntie................mx 147357-1

ALABAMA SACRED HARP SINGERS

15349-D..(Oct 29, 1928)
Religion Is A Fortune............................mx 147329-2
Cuba...mx 147330-2

15274-D..(Apr 16, 1928)
Rocky Road..mx 146091-2
Present Joys.......................................mx 146092-2

ALBERTVILLE QUARTET

15666-D..(Nov 5, 1929)
Workers For Jesus...............................mx 149387-2
I Hold This Hand..................................mx 149388-2

ALCOA QUARTET

15022-D.. (Jan 29, 1925)
Throw Out The Life Line........................mx 140294-2
Shall We Gather At The River..................mx 140295-2

ALLEN BROTHERS

15175-D..(Apr 7, 1927)
Salty Dog Blues...................................mx 143929-2
Bow Wow Blues...................................mx 143930-2

15270-D..(Apr 20, 1928)
Ain't That Skippin' And Flyin'..................mx 146150-2
Cheat 'Em..mx 146151-1

THE ARKANSAS WOODCHOPPER

15463-D..(Dec 6, 1928)
The Cowboy's Dream............................mx 147585-1
The Dying Cowboy................................mx 147586-1

CLARENCE ASHLEY

15489-D..(Oct 23, 1929)
Dark Holler Blues.................................mx 149250-2
The Coo – Coo Bird..............................mx 149251-2

CLARENCE ASHLEY

15522-D..(Oct 23, 1929)
Little Sadie......................................mx 149252-2
Naomi Wise....................................mx 149253-2

15654-D..(Apr 14, 1930)
The House Carpenter......................mx 150210-1
Old John Hardy...............................mx 150211-1

BEN BARTON & His ORCHESTRA
15744-D..(Jan 27, 1932)
The Bells Of Avalon........................mx 152090-?
Girl Of My Dreams..........................mx 152091-?

BANJO JOE (Willard Hodgin)
15238-D..(Feb 29, 1928)
Engineer Joe....................................mx 145696-2
I'm Just A Ramblin' Gambler..........mx 145697-2

BATEMAN SACRED QUARTET
15608-D..(Oct 23, 1929)
Nothing Like Old Time Religion....mx 149244-2
Some Day..mx 149245-1

THE BENTLEY BOYS
15565-D..(Oct 23, 1929)
Down on Penny's Farm...................mx 149254-2
Henhouse Blues...............................mx 149255-2

L.O. BIRKHEAD & R.M. LANE
15757-D..(Oct 25, 1931)
Robinson County.............................mx 151928-1
Cash river Waltz..............................mx 151929-1

BLALOCK & YATES (see Ira & Eugene Yates)
15576-D..(Oct 21, 1929)
Morning Star Waltz.........................mx 149200-2
Pride Of The Ball............................mx 149201-2

FRANK BLEVINS & HIS TAR HEEL RATTLERS
15210-D..(Nov 8, 1927)
Fly Around My Pretty Little Miss...mx 145163-2
Old Aunt Betsy...............................mx 145160-2

GREEN B. ADAIR

15166-D..(Mar 26, 1927)
Talkin' About My Gal...........................mx 143777-2
A Trip To The City................................mx 143778-1

15316-D..(Nov 9, 1927)
Lucy Wants Insurance...........................mx 145190-2
Malinda Gets Married............................mx 145191-3

AKINS BIRMINGHAM BOYS

15348-D..(Oct 31, 1928)
I Walked And Walked............................mx 147356-2
There Ain't No Flies On Auntie................mx 147357-1

ALABAMA SACRED HARP SINGERS

15349-D..(Oct 29, 1928)
Religion Is A Fortune............................mx 147329-2
Cuba...mx 147330-2

15274-D..(Apr 16, 1928)
Rocky Road...mx 146091-2
Present Joys..mx 146092-2

ALBERTVILLE QUARTET

15666-D..(Nov 5, 1929)
Workers For Jesus................................mx 149387-2
I Hold This Hand..................................mx 149388-2

ALCOA QUARTET

15022-D.. (Jan 29, 1925)
Throw Out The Life Line........................mx 140294-2
Shall We Gather At The River..................mx 140295-2

ALLEN BROTHERS

15175-D..(Apr 7, 1927)
Salty Dog Blues...................................mx 143929-2
Bow Wow Blues...................................mx 143930-2

15270-D..(Apr 20, 1928)
Ain't That Skippin' And Flyin'..................mx 146150-2
Cheat 'Em...mx 146151-1

THE ARKANSAS WOODCHOPPER

15463-D..(Dec 6, 1928)
The Cowboy's Dream............................mx 147585-1
The Dying Cowboy...............................mx 147586-1

CLARENCE ASHLEY

15489-D..(Oct 23, 1929)
Dark Holler Blues.................................mx 149250-2
The Coo – Coo Bird..............................mx 149251-2

CLARENCE ASHLEY

15522-D..(Oct 23, 1929)
Little Sadie..mx 149252-2
Naomi Wise.....................................mx 149253-2

15654-D..(Apr 14, 1930)
The House Carpenter.........................mx 150210-1
Old John Hardy.................................mx 150211-1

BEN BARTON & His ORCHESTRA
15744-D..(Jan 27, 1932)
The Bells Of Avalon...........................mx 152090-?
Girl Of My Dreams.............................mx 152091-?

BANJO JOE (Willard Hodgin)
15238-D..(Feb 29, 1928)
Engineer Joe......................................mx 145696-2
I'm Just A Ramblin' Gambler................mx 145697-2

BATEMAN SACRED QUARTET
15608-D..(Oct 23, 1929)
Nothing Like Old Time Religion............mx 149244-2
Some Day..mx 149245-1

THE BENTLEY BOYS
15565-D..(Oct 23, 1929)
Down on Penny's Farm.......................mx 149254-2
Henhouse Blues..................................mx 149255-2

L.O. BIRKHEAD & R.M. LANE
15757-D..(Oct 25, 1931)
Robinson County................................mx 151928-1
Cash river Waltz.................................mx 151929-1

BLALOCK & YATES (see Ira & Eugene Yates)
15576-D..(Oct 21, 1929)
Morning Star Waltz.............................mx 149200-2
Pride Of The Ball................................mx 149201-2

FRANK BLEVINS & HIS TAR HEEL RATTLERS
15210-D..(Nov 8, 1927)
Fly Around My Pretty Little Miss..........mx 145163-2
Old Aunt Betsy...................................mx 145160-2

FRANK BLEVINS & HIS TAR HEEL RATTLERS

15280-D..(Apr 17, 1928)
Don't Get Trouble In Your Mind...............mx 146104-1
Nine Pound Hammer...........................mx 146105-1

15765-D..(Nov 8, 1927)

Sally Ann...mx145158-2
I've Got No Honey Babe Now.................mx 145159-1

BLUE RIDGE HIGHBALLERS

15096-D..(Mar 24, 1926)
Going Down To Lynchburg Town............mx 141856-1
See Luther B. Clarke 15096-D

15070-D..(Mar 23, 1926)
Under The Double Eagle........................mx 141848-1
Green Mountain Polka...........................mx 141841-2

Blue Ridge Highballers Cont.

15081-D..(Mar 23, 1926)
Flop Eared Mule.................................mx 141843-1
Fourteen Days In Georgia.......................mx 141849-2

15089-D..(Mar 23, 1926)
Sandy River Belle................................mx 141850-2
Round Town Girls................................mx 141851-2

15132-D..(Mar 23, 1926)
Darneo...mx 141844-2
Darling Child.....................................mx 141846-1

15168-D..(Mar 23, 1926)
Skidd More.......................................mx 141842-2
Soldier's Joy......................................mx 141845-2
See Luther B. Clarke

BLUE RIDGE MOUNTAIN SINGERS

15550-D..(Apr 21, 1930)
I'll remember You Love In My Prayers.......mx 150333-2
Lorena..mx 150334-2

15580-D..(Apr 21, 1930)
Give My Love To Nell...........................mx 150321-?
The Letter That Never Came...................mx 150324-2

BLUE RIDGE MOUNTAIN SINGERS

15647-D..(Apr 21, 1930)
The Engineer's Last Run.......................mx 150322-1
The Tramp Song................................mx 150326-1

15678-D..(Apr 21, 1930)
Sinful To Flirt....................................mx 150323-1
Mansion Of Aching Hearts....................mx 150325-2

BLUE RIDGE SINGERS

15228-D..(Nov 5, 1927)
Glory Is Now Rising In My Soul..............mx 145121-1
I Want To Go There Don't You..............mx 145120-2

BENNY BORG

15148-D..(Apr 2, 1927)
I Want A Pardon For My Daddy..............mx 143860-1
You're Going To Leave The Old Home Jim Tonight
....mx 143862-1

15183-D..(Apr 2, 1927)
Picture From Life's Other Side................mx 143859-2
Concert Hall On The Bowery..................mx 143861-2

LEO BOSWELL (Leo & Dewey Boswell)

15290-D..(Apr 14, 1928)
Two Little Girls In Blue........................mx 146081-2
The Fatal Rose Of Red........................mx 146082-2

15469-D..(Apr 14, 1928)
A Memory That Time Cannot Erase..........mx 146083-2
I Love You Nellie...............................mx 146084-1
See Elzie Floyd & Merritt Smith

CHRIS BOUCHILLON

15120-D..(Nov 4, 1926)
Talking Blues....................................mx 143060-2
Hannah...mx 143061-1

15151-D..(Apr 5, 1927)
Born In Hard Luck..............................mx 143898-2
Medicine Show..................................mx 143899-2

15178-D
Let It Alone.....................mx 143772-2 / Mar 26, 1927
My Fat Girl......................mx 143897-3 / Apr 5, 1927

CHRIS BOUCHILLON

15213-D..(Nov 10, 1927)
Chris Visits The Barber Shop....................mx 145208-2
Bullfight In Mexico..............................mx 145209-2

15244-D..(Mar 26, 1927)
Waltz Me Around Again Willie mx..................143771-2
You Look Awful Good To Me..................mx 143773-1

15262-D..(Apr 16, 1928)
Old Blind Heck..................................mx 146085-1
New Talking Blues..............................mx 146086-1

15289-D..(Apr 16, 1928)
I've Been Married Three Times.................mx 146088-1
My Wife's Wedding............................mx 146089-2

15317-D..(Apr 16, 1928)
I Got Mine..mx 146087-2
Oyster Stew......................................mx 146090-2

15345-D (as by Mr. & Mrs. Chris Bouchillon)
....(Oct 29, 1928)
Adam And Eve Part 1............................mx 147333-2
Adam And Eve Part 2............................mx 147334-2

15373-D..(Oct 30, 1928)
Speed Maniac.....................................mx 147339-2
Ambitious Father................................mx 147340-1

15508-D..(Oct 30, 1928)
Girls Of To–Day.................................mx 147341-2
Oh Miss Lizzie..................................mx 147342-2

CHARLIE BOWMAN & His BROTHERS
15357-D..(Oct 16, 1928)
Roll On Buddy...................................mx 147208-2
Gonna Raise The Ruckus Tonight..............mx 147209-2

15387-D..(Feb 20, 1929)
Forky Dear..mx 147972-2
Moonshiner And His Money...................mx 147973-1

BOWMAN SISTERS
15473-D..(Oct 16, 1928)
My Old Kentucky Home.......................mx 147206-2
Swanee River....................................mx 147207-2

BOWMAN SISTERS
15621-D..(Oct 23, 1929)
Railroad Take Me Back..........................mx 149256-2
Old Lonesome Blues.............................mx 149257-2

BROCK & DUDLEY
15645-D..(Apr 23, 1930)
I'll Remember You Love........................mx 150368-1
Lonely..mx 150369-2

BOB BROOKES (Bob McGimsey)
15676-D..(May 18, 1931)
Shadrach...mx 151555-3
Wandering Lamb..................................mx 151556-1

15689-D..(June 19, 1931)
Red River Valley..................................mx 151619-3
Lonesome Cowboy...............................mx 151620-2

BILLY BROOKS
15614-D..(Apr 16, 1930)
Freight Train Blues...............................mx 150241-2
Just From College.................................mx 150242-2

CHARLES S. BROOK & CHARLIE TURNER
15756-D..(Nov 2, 1931)
Mama I Wish I'd Listened To You............mx 152009-1
Will You Love Me When I'm Old..............mx 152010-1

CHARLES BROOKS
15733-D..(Oct 29, 1931)
My Mammy's Cabin..............................mx 151984-1
Baby..mx 151985-1

BUICE BROTHERS
15527-D..(Apr 19, 1928)
The Home-Coming Week.......................mx 146146-2
I'm His At Last....................................mx 146147-2

BURNETT & RUTHERFORD
15113-D..(Nov 6, 1926)
Weeping Willow Tree............................mx 143094-1
Pearl Bryan...mx 143097-1

15122-D..(Nov 6, 1926)
I'll Be With You When The Roses Bloom Again
....mx 143095-2
Lost John..mx 143092-2

CHRIS BOUCHILLON

15213-D..(Nov 10, 1927)
Chris Visits The Barber Shop....................mx 145208-2
Bullfight In Mexico.............................mx 145209-2

15244-D..(Mar 26, 1927)
Waltz Me Around Again Willie mx..................143771-2
You Look Awful Good To Me...................mx 143773-1

15262-D..(Apr 16, 1928)
Old Blind Heck..................................mx 146085-1
New Talking Blues..............................mx 146086-1

15289-D..(Apr 16, 1928)
I've Been Married Three Times.................mx 146088-1
My Wife's Wedding............................mx 146089-2

15317-D..(Apr 16, 1928)
I Got Mine......................................mx 146087-2
Oyster Stew.....................................mx 146090-2

15345-D (as by Mr. & Mrs. Chris Bouchillon)
....(Oct 29, 1928)
Adam And Eve Part 1...........................mx 147333-2
Adam And Eve Part 2...........................mx 147334-2

15373-D..(Oct 30, 1928)
Speed Maniac...................................mx 147339-2
Ambitious Father...............................mx 147340-1

15508-D..(Oct 30, 1928)
Girls Of To–Day................................mx 147341-2
Oh Miss Lizzie..................................mx 147342-2

CHARLIE BOWMAN & His BROTHERS
15357-D..(Oct 16, 1928)
Roll On Buddy..................................mx 147208-2
Gonna Raise The Ruckus Tonight.............mx 147209-2

15387-D..(Feb 20, 1929)
Forky Dear.......................................mx 147972-2
Moonshiner And His Money...................mx 147973-1

BOWMAN SISTERS
15473-D..(Oct 16, 1928)
My Old Kentucky Home......................mx 147206-2
Swanee River...................................mx 147207-2

BOWMAN SISTERS
15621-D..(Oct 23, 1929)
Railroad Take Me Back..........................mx 149256-2
Old Lonesome Blues..............................mx 149257-2

BROCK & DUDLEY
15645-D..(Apr 23, 1930)
I'll Remember You Love.........................mx 150368-1
Lonely...mx 150369-2

BOB BROOKES (Bob McGimsey)
15676-D..(May 18, 1931)
Shadrach..mx 151555-3
Wandering Lamb...................................mx 151556-1

15689-D..(June 19, 1931)
Red River Valley...................................mx 151619-3
Lonesome Cowboy................................mx 151620-2

BILLY BROOKS
15614-D..(Apr 16, 1930)
Freight Train Blues................................mx 150241-2
Just From College..................................mx 150242-2

CHARLES S. BROOK & CHARLIE TURNER
15756-D..(Nov 2, 1931)
Mama I Wish I'd Listened To You............mx 152009-1
Will You Love Me When I'm Old.............mx 152010-1

CHARLES BROOKS
15733-D..(Oct 29, 1931)
My Mammy's Cabin..............................mx 151984-1
Baby..mx 151985-1

BUICE BROTHERS
15527-D..(Apr 19, 1928)
The Home-Coming Week.......................mx 146146-2
I'm His At Last.....................................mx 146147-2

BURNETT & RUTHERFORD
15113-D..(Nov 6, 1926)
Weeping Willow Tree.............................mx 143094-1
Pearl Bryan..mx 143097-1

15122-D..(Nov 6, 1926)
I'll Be With You When The Roses Bloom Again
....mx 143095-2
Lost John...mx 143092-2

BURNETT & RUTHERFORD

15133-D..(Nov 6, 1926)
Little Stream Of Whiskey........................mx 143093-2
Short Life Of Trouble............................mx 143096-1

15187-D..(Apr 2, 1927)
Are You Happy Or Lonesome..................mx 143874-2
My Sweetheart In Tennessee...................mx 143873-2

15209-D..(Nov 3, 1927)
Ladies On A Steamboat.........................mx 145088-1
Billy In The Low Ground.......................mx 145089-2

15240-D..(Nov 3, 1927)
Curley Headed Woman..........................mx 145084-2
Ramblin' Reckless Hobo........................mx 145085-1

15314-D..(Nov 3, 1927)
Willie Moore......................................mx 145086-1
All Night Long Blues............................mx 145087-2

15567-D..(Apr 19, 1930)
Sleeping Lulu.....................................mx 150293-2
Blackberry Blossoms............................mx 150294-1

JEWELL BURNS & CHARLIE D. TILLMAN

15026-D.. (Jan 27, 1925)
Sometime Somewhere...........................mx 140291-1
Tell It Again......................................mx 140290-2

15024-D.. (Jan 27, 1925)
Someday, It Won't Be Long....................mx 140283-1
Old Time Power..................................mx 140282-1

15025-D.. (Jan 27, 1925)
My Mother's Bible...............................mx 140284-2
Don't Forget The Old Folks.....................mx 140285-1

BUSH FAMILY (BUSH BROTHERS)

15157-D..(Apr 12, 1927)
Music In My Soul...............................mx 143960-2
On My Way To Jesus............................mx 143962-2

15203-D **(as by Bush Brothers)**..............(Oct 27, 1927)
Saved By His Sweet Grace......................mx 145029-2
He Pardoned Me..................................mx 145030-2

15235-D..(Oct 27, 1927)
Hallelujah! He Is Mine..........................mx 145031-1
Oh Wonderful Day...............................mx 145032-1

BUSH FAMILY (BUSH BROTHERS)
15263-D **(as by Bush Brothers)**............ (Apr 26, 1928)
When The Gates Of Glory Open...............mx 146196-2
On The Glory Road...............................mx 146197-2

15287-D **(as by Bush Brothers)**...............(Apr 26, 1928)
Does Your Path Seem Long.....................mx 146203-2
Complete For All The World...................mx 146204-1

15368-D **(as by Bush Brothers)**...............(Oct 27, 1927)
Mother Dear Is Waiting..........................mx 145033-2
Called Home......................................mx 145034-1

15500-D **(as by Bush Brothers)**.............(Dec 10, 1929)
Endless Glory To the Lamb.....................mx 149570-2
My Happiest Day.................................mx 149571-2

15524-D **(as by Bush Brothers)**.............(Dec 10, 1929)
Keep Your Light Shining........................mx 149574-1
The Pathway......................................mx 149575-2

15696-D **(as by Bush Brothers)**.............(Dec 18, 1930)
What Love..mx 151129-2
I'm No Stranger To Jesus........................mx 151130-2

15649-D **(as by Bush Brothers)**.............(Dec 18, 1930)
A Look Inside The Glory Gate..................mx 151127-2
I'll Make It My Home............................mx 151128-2

WALLACE BUTLER HOTEL DeSOTA ORHESTRA
15018-D... (Jan 1925)
Doo Wacka Doo ....mx 140292
I Wonder If You Still Love Me..................mx 140293

CALIFORNIA AEOLIANS
15699-D...(July 1931)
The Rose Of Sharon..............................mx 151673-2
The Old Rugged Cross...........................mx 151677-2

CANOVA FAMILY
15630-D **(as by Three Georgia Crackers)**
....(Dec 18, 1930)
I've Been Hoodooed..............................mx 151159-3
Whoa, Buck, Whoa...............................mx 151165-2

15653-D **(as by Three Georgia Crackers)**
Poor Little Thing Cried Mammy
....mx 151160-2 / Dec 18, 1930
Hannah, My Love...............mx 151168-2 / Dec 19, 1930

CAROLINA BUDDIES

15537-D……………………………..(Mar 25, 1930)
The Murder Of The Lawson Family………..mx 150114-1
In A Cottage By The Sea…………………mx 150115-1

15641-D……………………………..(Mar 25, 1930)
The Story That The Crow Told…..Me……..mx 150116-1
My Sweetheart Is A Sly Little Miss…………mx 150117-1

15652-D……………………………..(Feb 24, 1931)
Otto Wood The Bandit……………………mx 151345-2
Broken Hearted Lover……………………mx 151346-2

15663-D……………………………..(Feb 24, 1931)
Work Don't Bother Me……………………mx 151340-2
He Went In Like A Lion (But Came Out Like A Lamb)
………………………………………mx 151341-2

15770-D……………………………..(Feb 24, 1931)
My Evolution Girl…………………….....mx 151344-2
Mistreated Blues…………………………mx 151347-2

BUSTER CARTER & PRESTON YOUNG

15690-D……………………………..(June 26, 1931)
It's Hard To Love And Can't Be Loved…….mx 151643-2
I'll Roll In My Sweet Baby's Arms…………mx 151651-1

15702-D……………………………..(June 26, 1931)
It Won't hurt No More……………………mx 151647-1
A Lazy Farmer Boy………………………mx 151648-2

15758-D……………………………..(June 26, 1931)
What Sugar Head Licker Will Do…………..mx 151649-1
Bill Morgan And His Gal…………………mx 151650-1

CARTWRIGHT BROTHERS

15220-D……………………………..(Dec 2, 1927)
Kelley Waltz……………………………mx 145300-2
Honeymoon Waltz………………………mx 145301-3

15346-D……………………………..(Dec 6, 1928)
When The Work's All Done This Fall………mx 147578-2
On The Old Chisholm Trail………………mx 147578-2

15410-D……………………………..(Dec. 6, 1929)
Get Along Little Dogies…………………mx 147579-2
Utah Carrol……………………………mx 147580-2

CARTWRIGHT BROTHERS
15677-D
Over The Waves……………..mx 147581-? / Dec 6, 1928
See Bob Ferguson (Bob Miller) 15677-D

ELRY CASH
15399-D……………………………….(Apr 18, 1929)
My Old New Hampshire Home……………mx 148348-2
Won't You Come Back to Me……………mx 148349-1

15457-D……………………………….(Apr 18, 1929)
Then My Love Began To Wane……………mx 148350-2
When You're In The graveyard And I'm Away
Downtown In Jail……………………..mx 148351-2

W.C. CHILDERS
15728-D **(as by Warner & Jenkins)**
………………………………………..(Oct 24, 1931)
A Sweetheart's Promise………………..mx 151922-1
When The Dew Is On The Rose……………mx 151923-1

THE CHUMBLER FAMILY
15481-D……………………………….(Nov 4, 1929)
Sailing To Glory……………………...mx 149359-2
Jaobs Ladder………………………...mx 149360-2

15513-D……………………………….(Nov 4, 1929)
I'm Going Home To My Wife……………..mx 149362-2
If He Should Come Again………………..mx 149963-1

LUTHER B. CLARKE
15069-D **(as by Luther B. Clarke With The Blue Ridge Highballers)**
…………………………………..................(Mar 24, 1926)
Bright Sherman Valley………………...mx 141853-2
I'll Be All Smiles To-night…………………mx 141854-1

15096-D **(as by Luther B. Clarke)**
…………………………………….......(Mar 24, 1926)
Wish To The Lord I Have Never Been Born
……………………………………………mx 141855-2
See Blue Ridge Highballers 15096-D

CLASSIC CITY QUARTET
15566-D……………………………….(Nov 6, 1929)
I'll Be Singing 'Round The Throne Someday
……………………………………………mx 149389-2
Hold Thou To Me……………………...mx 149390-2

COLUMBIA BAND
15782-D..............................……......(June 21, 1929)
Anchors Aweigh.................................mx 148748-?
See Bob Ferguson (Bob Miller) 15782-D

CARL CONNER
15076-D...(Apr 23, 1926)
Jones & Bloodworth Case........................mx 142092-1
Story Of Gerald Chapman......................mx 142093--3

HERB COOK
15729-D...(Oct 27, 1931)
Arkansaw Sweetheart............................mx 151962-2
Lou'siana..mx 151964-2

15778-D...(Oct 27, 1931)
I Wonder Why....................................mx 151963-1
Just A Little Happiness..........................mx 151965-1

COPPERHILL MALE QUARTET / THE HAPPY FOUR
15164-D..(Apr 6, 1927)
There Is A Fountain Filled With Blood........mx 143925-2
(see 15225-D The Happy Four)

THE CORLEY FAMILY
15495-D..(Dec 4, 1929)
He Keeps My Soul...............................mx 149518-2
When Jesus Comes..............................mx 149519-2

15574-D..(Dec 4, 1929)
The Way To Glory Land........................mx 149520-1
Give The World A Smile........................mx 149521-2

COWBOY TOM'S ROUNDUP With CHIEF SHUNATONA, DOUG McTAGUE & SKOOKUM
15781-D...(Sept 19, 1932)
Cowboy Tom's Roundup Part 1 Get Along Little Doggies;The Dawn; Cowboy's Trademarks
....mx 152300-1
Cowboy Tom's Roundup Part 2 Red River Valley; Tom Tom Dance; Going Back to Texas.............mx 152301-1

EDWARD L. CRAIN (The Texas Cowboy)
15710-D...(Aug 17, 1931)
Bandit Cole Younger............................mx 151731-2
Cowboy's Home Sweet Home..................mx 151733-2

AL CRAVER
See Vernon Dalhart

CROSS & McCARTT (Hugh Cross & Luther McCartt)

15143-D..(Apr 7, 1927)
When The Roses Bloom Again.................mx 143931-1
Sweet Rosie O'Grady............................mx 143932-2

HUGH CROSS

15182-D..(Apr 7, 1927)
I'm Going Away From The Cotton Fields......mx 143934-2
The Parlor Is A Pleasant Place To Sit..........mx 143933-1

15206-D (Hugh Cross & RileyPuckett)
....(Nov 3, 1927)
Red River Valley................................mx 145091-2
When You Wore A Tulip........................mx 145092-1

15231-D..(Nov 2, 1927)
Down Where The Cotton Blossoms Grow....mx 145070-1
Mansion Of Aching Hearts......................mx 145071-2

15259-D (as by Mr. & Mrs. Hugh Cross)
....(Apr 11, 1928)
I Love You Best Of All..........................mx 146008-2
You're As Welcome As The Flowers In May
....mx 146009-1

15266-D (Hugh Cross & Riley Puckett)
....(Apr 12, 1928)
Where The Morning Glory Grows.............mx 146028-2
My Wild Irish Rose.............................mx 146029-1

15337-D (Hugh Cross & Riley Puckett)
Call Me Back Pal O' Mine...mx 147244-2 / Oct 22, 1928
Clover Blossoms...............mx 147265-2 / Oct 23, 1928

15365-D..(Oct 23, 1928)
In The Hills Of Tennessee.......................mx 147259-2
Never No More Blues...........................mx 147260-1

15395-D (as by Mr. & Mrs. Hugh Cross)
....(Apr 8, 1928)
Dearest Sweetest Mother........................mx 148204-2
Mother's Plea....................................mx 148205-2

HUGH CROSS

15421-D (Hugh Cross & Riley Puckett)
Tuck Me To Sleep In My Old Kentucky Home
……………………………….mx 146026-2 / Apr 12, 1928
Go Feather Your Nest………..mx 148230-1 / Apr 10 1929

15439-D………………………………………..(Apr 9, 1929)
I'll Climb The Blue Ridge Mountains Back To You
……………………………………………….mx 148218-2
Wabash Cannon Ball………………………..mx 148219-1

15455-D (Hugh Cross & Riley Puckett)
Gonna Raise Ruckus Tonight
………………………………….mx 146027-2 / Apr 12, 1928
I'm Going To Settle Down
………………………………….mx 148229-1 / Apr 29, 1929

15458-D (as by Mr. & Mrs. Hugh Cross)
………………………………………………..(Apr 8, 1929)
Down Where The Swanee River Flows………mx148206-2
Pretty Little Blue-Eyed Sally…………………..mx 148207-2

15478-D (Hugh Cross & Riley Puckett)
…………………………………………………..(Oct 23, 1928)
Smiles……………………………………..mx 147266-1
Tell Me……………………………………mx 147267-2

(15482-D See Clayton McMichen)

15504-D (as by Mr. & Mrs. Hugh Cross)
………………………………………………..(Oct 29,1929)
My Old Cabin Home…………………...mx 149284-2
When The Flowers Bloom Again In The Ozarks
……………………………………………….mx 149285-1

15575-D (as by Mr. & Mrs. Hugh Cross)
There's A Mother Old And Gray
…………………………………mx 149291-2 / Oct 29, 1929
When The Bees Are In The Hive
………………………………….mx 149292-1 / Oct 30, 1929

15613-D (as by Mr. & Mrs. Hugh Cross)
………………………………………………..(Apr 11, 1928)
If I Had Only Had A Home Sweet Home…....mx 146010-2
My Little Home In Tennessee ……………...mx 146011-2

VERNON DALHART

15028-D... (Apr 6, 1925)
In The Baggage Coach Ahead.................mx 140407-4
A Boy's Best Friend Is His Mother............mx 140408-3

15030-D... (May 13, 1925)
The Picture That Is Turned Toward The Wall
....mx 140595-3
After The Ball.................................mx 140596-2

15031-D **(as by Al Craver)**...................(May 27, 1925)
Death Of Floyd Collins..........................mx 140627-3
Little Mary Phagan..............................mx 140628-1

15032-D... (June 4, 1925)
Sinking Of The Titanic........................mx W140646-2
New River Train................................mx W140647-1

15034-D **(as by Al Craver)**
Roving Gambler.................mx W140656 / June 6, 1925
Wreck Of The 1256...... mx W140708 / June 22, 1925

15037-D... (July 10, 1925)
Santa Barbara Earthquake.....................mx W140679-3
The John T Scopes Trial......................mx W140680-1

15039-D... (Aug 10, 1925)
William J Bryan's Last Flight.................mx W140831-3
Many Many Years Ago........................mx W140832-1

15041-D...(Sept 11, 1925)
Wreck Of The Shenandoah...................mx W140929-1
Stone Mountain Memorial....................mx W140930-1

15042-D
Frank Dupree.................mx W140931-2 / Sept 11, 1924
Sydney Allen.................mx W140967-2 / Sept 19, 1924

15044-D **(as by Al Craver)**
Sinking Of Submarine S51...mx W141099-2 / Oct 9, 1925
Little Birdie................mx W141018-1 / Sept 19, 1925

15046-D **(as by AL Craver)**................. (Oct 17, 1925)
The Convict And The Rose...................mx W141151-1
Dream Of A Miner's Child...................mx W141152-1

VERNON DALHART

15048-D
Mother's Grave…………...mx W140932-1 / Sept 11, 1925
Curse Of An Aching Heart
………………………...mx W140966-2 / Sept 19, 1925

15049-D **(as by Al Craver)**…………......(Nov 4, 1925)
Letter Edged In Black……………..……mx W141239-1
Zeb Turney's Girl…………………….…mx W141240-3

15051-D………………………………….(Oct 17, 1925)
The Fatal Wedding………………….…..mx W141149-1
The Dying Girl's Message……………....mx W141150-1

15053-D **(as by Al Craver)**……..………..(Nov 24, 1925)
Thomas E Watson……………………....mx W141314-2
Naomi Wise…………………….............mx W141313-2

15054-D……………………………….… (Dec 8, 1925)
Mollie Darling………………….............mx W141364-2
I'll Be With You When The Roses Bloom Again
……………………………………..........mx W141365-3

15056-D **(as by Al Craver)**
My Little Home In Tennessee
………………………….mx W141312-2 / Nov 24, 1925
Unknown Soldiers Grave
…………………………..mx W141363-2 / Dec 8, 1925

15060-D **(as by Al Craver / Vernon Dalhart)**
The Engineer's Dying Child
……………………………..mx141495-1 / Jan 15, 1926
Sentenced To Life Behind These Grey Walls
…………………………...mx 141311-1 / Nov 24, 1925

15062-D……………………………........(Jan 15, 1926)
Down On The Farm………………….....mx 141497--2
My Mother's Old Red Shawl……………..mx 141498-2

15064-D………………………….............(Feb 16, 1926)
      (as by Dalhart Texas Panhandlers)
Better Get Out Of My Way……………....mx 141636-1
Death Of The Floyd Collins………….......mx 141637-1

15065-D **(as by Al Craver)**
Freight Wreck At Altoona
………………………….mx 141496-2 / Jan 15, 1926
Kinnie Wagner……………..mx 141638-1 / Feb 16, 1926

VERNON DALHART

15066-D... (Mar 3, 1926)
Guy Massey's Farewell..........................mx 141749-1
The Prison Clock....................................mx 141750-1

15072-D..(Feb 16, 1926)
Where Is My Wandering Boy Tonight.........mx 141639-2
He Will Lead Me Home..........................mx 141640-2

15077-D..(Apr 13, 1926)
Little Black Mustache.............................mx 141956-2
Old Bill Moser's Ford.............................mx 141957-2

15082-D...(Apr 5, 1926)
Goin' To Have A Big Time Tonight...........mx 141914-2
Putting On The Style..............................mx 141915-1

15086-D **(as by Al Craver)**...................(June 25, 1926)
John The Baptist....................................mx 142346-2
The Tramp..mx 142347-2

15087-D...(June 29, 1926)
Old Fiddlers Song..................................mx 142357-1
Lay My Head Beneath A Rose.................mx 142358-2

15092D...(Aug 4, 1926)
Picnic In The Wildwood.........................mx 142499-2
On That Dixie Bee Line..........................mx 142507-3

15098-D **(as by Al Craver)**...................(Sept 14, 1926)
Billy Richardson's Last Ride....................mx 142617-3
Kinnie Wagner's Surrender.....................mx 142616-3

15100-D...(Sept 23, 1926)
Miami Storm..mx 142683-1
An Old Fashioned Picture.......................mx 142684-1

15107-D...(Oct 23, 1926)
The Crepe On The Little Cabin Door..........mx 142866-3
We Will Meet At The End Of The Trail.......mx 142867-1

15109-D (as by Al Craver w/ Charlie Wells)
....(Nov 8, 1926)
Fate Of Kinnie Wagner...........................mx 142922-3
We Sat Beneath The Maple On The Hill......mx 142923-2

VERNON DALHART

15121-D **(as by Al Craver)**....................(Jan 14, 1927)
Wreck Of The Number Nine....................mx 143308-3
Wreck Of The Royal Palm Express............mx 143309-2

15126-D (as by Al Craver).......................(Feb 3, 1927)
Barbara Allen.......................................mx 143385-3
Three Drowned Sisters..........................mx 143384-3

15131-D
I'd Like To Be Back In Texas
......................................mx 142895-2 / Nov 1, 1926
The Sad Lover...................mx 143310-2 / Jan 14, 1927

15135-D **(w/ Charlie Wells)**.............(Mar 1, 1927)
Billy The Kid................................mx 143554-2
Wreck Of The C & O Number 5.........mx 143555-3

15146-D **(as by Al Craver)**...................(May 2, 1927)
Mississippi Flood................................mx 144075-2
The Engineer's Dream..........................mx 144076-1

15152-D **(w/ Charlie Wells)**.............(Mar 1, 1927)
My Blue Ridge Mountain Home
....................................mx 143557-3 Mar 1927
Death's Shadow Song ....mx 143556-3

15162-D **(w/ Charlie Wells)**
The Airship That Never Returned
......................................mx 144210-2 / May 24, 1927
I Know There Is Somebody Waiting
......................................mx 143386-2 / Feb 3, 1927

15169-D **(as by Al Craver)**
Pearl Bryan......................mx 142896-2 / Nov 1, 1926
Death Of Lura Parsons........mx 144211-1 / May 24, 1927

15181-D **(w/ Charlie Wells)**..................(Aug 29, 1927)
When The Moon Shines Down On The Mountain
....mx 144589-2
Golden Slippers...................................mx 144590-2

15192-D **(as by Al Craver)**...................(Sept 15, 1927)
The Fate Of Mildred Doran.....................mx 144676-3
Jim Blake The Engineer..........................mx 144677-3

VERNON DALHART

15218-D (as by Al Craver w/ Charlie Wells)
Where Is My Mama................mx 145474-1 / Jan 4, 1928
Little Marian Parker...........mx 145475-3 / Jan 5, 1928

15223-D (as by Al Craver w/ Charlie Wells)
....(Jan 25, 1928)
Good Old Country Town......................mx 145581-2
Henry's Made A Lady Out Of Lizzie..........mx 145582-1

15251-D (as by Al Craver w/ Charlie Wells)
....(Apr 5, 1928)
Hanging Of The Fox.........................mx 145963-2
Six Feet Of Earth..........................mx 145966-3

15256-D (as by Al Craver) / Carolina Night Hawks
The Sidewalks Of New York (East Side, West Side)
...............................mx 140795-2 / July 30, 1925
Governor Al Smith For President
.............................mx 146119-1 / Apr 17, 1928

15265-D Vernon Dalhart / Vernon Dalhart & Carson Robison ....(June 2, 1928)
Climbing Up De Golden Stairs................mx 146382-2
Steamboat Keep Rockin'......................mx 146383-2

15282-D (w/ Carson Robison).................(Apr 5, 1928)
Drifting Down The Trail Of Dreams..........mx 145964-3
Bring Me A Leaf From The Sea...............mx 145965-3

15302-D..(Sept 11, 1928)
Bully Song Part 1..............................mx 146980-2
Bully Song Part 2..............................mx 146981-3

15306-D (w/ Adelyne Hood).................(Sept 24, 1928)
Sing Hallelujah................................mx 147053-1
The Frog Song..................................mx 147054-3

15320-D..(Oct 9, 1928)
Santa Claus, That's Me.........................mx 147116-3
Hooray For St. Nick............................mx 147117-3

15343-D..(July 24, 1928)
The Ohio River Blues...........................mx 146789-2
'Er Somethin'..................................mx 146790-3

VERNON DALHART

15378-D..(Jan 16, 1929)
Wreck Of The Northwest Cannonball.........mx 147789-2
Low Bridge Everybody Down..................mx 147790-3

15386-D...(Mar 28, 1929)
The Alabama Flood............................mx 148143-3
Roll On River....................................mx 148144-2

15405-D..(May 9, 1929)
Ain't Gonna Grieve My Mind..................mx 148478-3
Poor Old Mare...................................mx 148488-2

15417-D (as by Adelyne Hood & Vernon Dalhart)
....(June 6, 1929)
Razor's In De Air...............................mx 148660-1
Dixie Way..mx 148661-2

15440-D...(July 22, 1929)
The Old Kitty Kate (On The Mississippi Line)
....mx 148836-3
Going Down To New Orleans..................mx 148837-3

15449-D (as by Al Craver)...................(Aug 22, 1929)
Farm relief Song................................mx 148913-2
The Crow Song Caw Caw Caw................mx 148914-3

15475-D...(Oct 24, 1929)
Home In The Mountains........................mx 149177-2
Blue Ridge Sweetheart..........................mx 149178-2

15512-D (as by Al Craver)....................(Jan 29, 1930)
Eleven More Months And Ten More Days
....mx 149925-3
Squint Eyed Catus Jones.......................mx 149926-2

15530-D (as by Al Craver)...................(Mar 6, 1930)
The Hanging Of Eva Dugan....................mx 150068-2
Pappy's Buried On The Hill....................mx 150069-3

15542-D (as by Vernon Dalhart / Vernon Dalhart & Adelyne Hood)..............................(Mar 31, 1930)
You Ain't Been Living Right..................mx 150152-1
Hallelujah, There's A Rainbow In The Sky
....mx 150151-3

VERNON DALHART

15546-D **(as by Al Craver)**...................(Mar 31, 1930)
For The First Time In Twenty Four Years
....mx 150149-2
In 1992..mx 150150-1

15561-D **(as by Al Craver)**...................(May 16, 1930)
The Tariff Bill Song............................mx 150433-3
My Oklahoma Home..........................mx 150436-3

15585-D **(as by Al Craver)**................(Sept 24, 1928)
Conversation With Death (A Blind Girl)
....mx 147051-1
The Old Bureau Drawer..................mx 147052-2

15610-D...(May 16, 1930)
My Mary Jane..................................mx 150434-3
The Deacon's Prayer.........................mx 150435-3

DANIELS –DEASON SACRED HARP SINGERS

15323-D..(Oct 24, 1928)
Primrose Hill.....................................mx 147280-2
Coronation..mx 147281-2

TOM DARBY & JIMMIE TARLTON (See Jimmie Tarlton)

15197-D **(as by Darby & Tarlton)**
....(Apr 5, 1927)
Down In Florida On A Hog.....................mx 143902-2
Birmingham Town..............................mx 143903-1

15212-D **(as by Darby & Tarlton)**
....(Nov 10, 1927)
Birmingham Jail................................mx 145202-2
Columbus StockadeBlues......................mx 145203-2

15254-D **(as by Darby & Tarlton)**
....(Apr 12, 1928)
After The Ball..................................mx 146042-2
I Can't Tell Why I Love You..................mx 146043-2

15293-D **(as by Darby & Tarlton)**
....(Apr 12, 1928)
The Irish Police.................................mx 146044-2
The Hobo Tramp................................mx 146045-2

TOM DARBY & JIMMIE TARLTON (See Jimmie Tarlton)

15319-D (as by Darby & Tarlton)
....(Apr 12, 1928)
Mexican Rag......................................mx 146049-2
Alto Waltz...mx 146046-2

15330-D (as by Tom Darby & Jimmie Tarlton)
....(Oct 28, 1928)
Traveling Yodel Blues..........................mx 147368-1
Heavy Hearted Blues...........................mx 147369-1

15360-D (as by Tom Darby & Jimmie Tarlton)
....(Oct 31, 1928)
Country Girl Valley.............................mx 147360-2
The Rainbow Division.........................mx 147359-2

15375-D (as by Tom Darby & Jimmie Tarlton)
....(Oct 31, 1928)
Birmingham Jail No. 2..........................mx 147358-2
Lonesome Railroad..............................mx 147361-2

15388-D (as by Tom Darby & Jimmie Tarlton)
....(Oct 31, 1928)
If You Ever Learn To Love Me................mx 147366-1
If I Had Listened To My Mother...............mx 147367-2

15403-D (as by Tom Darby & Jimmie Tarlton)
....(Apr 15, 1929)
Down In The Old Cherry Orchard.............mx 148303-2
When The Bluebirds Nest Again...............mx 148304-1

15419-D (as by Tom Darby & Jimmie Tarlton)
....(Apr 15, 1929)
Touring Yodeling Blues.........................mx 148295-2
Slow Wicked Blues..............................mx 148296-2

15436-D (as by Tom Darby & Jimmie Tarlton)
....(Apr 15, 1929)
Birmingham Rag.................................mx 148307-2
Sweet Sarah Blues...............................mx 148308-2

15452-D (as by Tom Darby & Jimmie Tarlton)
....(Apr 15, 1929)
The New York Hobo............................mx 148293-2
Black Jack Moonshine..........................mx 148297-2

TOM DARBY & JIMMIE TARLTON (See Jimmie Tarlton)

15477-D (as by Tom Darby & Jimmie Tarlton)
....(Apr 15, 1929)
All Bound Down To Texas.....................mx 148294-2
Ain't Gonna Mary No More...................mx 148298-1

15492-D (as by Tom Darby & Jimmie Tarlton)
....(Oct 31, 1929)
Little Bessie..mx 149309-1
I Left Her At The River.........................mx 149310-2

15511-D (as by Tom Darby & Jimmie Tarlton)
....(Oct 31, 1929)
The Whistling Songbird........................mx 149323-2
Freight Train Ramble............................mx 149324-2

15528-D (as by Tom Darby & Jimmie Tarlton)
....(Oct 31, 1929)
Jack And May.....................................mx 149311-2
Captain Won't You Let Me Go Home.........mx 149312-1

15552-D (as by Tom Darby & Jimmie Tarlton)
My Father Died A Drunkard
....................................mx 150251-2 / Apr 16, 1930
Faithless Husband..............mx 150265-2 / Apr 17, 1930

15572-D (as by Tom Darby & Jimmie Tarlton)
....(Apr 17, 1930)
On The Banks Of A Lonely River..............mx 150264-2
My Little Blue Heaven..........................mx 150268-2

15591-D (as by Tom Darby & Jimmie Tarlton)
....(Apr 16, 1930)
Little Ola..mx 150248-1
The Maple On The Hill.........................mx 150250-1

15611-D (as by Tom Darby & Jimmie Tarlton)
....(Apr 17, 1930)
Pork Chops.......................................mx 150263-1
Hard Time Blues.................................mx 150266-1

15624-D (as by Tom Darby & Jimmie Tarlton)
....(Apr 15, 1929)
Beggar Joe..mx 148305-2
When You're Far Away From Home..........mx 148306-2

TOM DARBY & JIMMIE TARLTON (See Jimmie Tarlton)

15674-D (as by Tom Darby & Jimmie Tarlton)
....(Apr 16, 1930)
The Black Sheep................................mx 150247-2
Once I Had A Sweetheart.......................mx 150249-2

15684-D (as by Darby & Tarlton)
....(Nov 10, 1927)
Gamblin' Jim......................................mx 145204-2
Lonesome In The Pines.........................mx 145205-2

15701-D (as by Tom Darby & Jimmie Tarlton)
Frankie Dean....................mx 150252-1 / Apr 16, 1930
Rising Sun Blues...............mx 150267-1 / Apr 17, 1930

15715-D (as by Tom Darby & Jimmie Tarlton)
....(Oct 31, 1929)
Going Back To My Texas Home...............mx 149322-1
Down Among The Sugar Cane.................mx 149326-1

CLAUDE DAVIS

15397-D (as by Claude Davis & Bob Nichols)
(See Clayton McMichen regarding Bob Nichols)
....(Apr 9, 1929)
We Were Pals Together.........................mx 148220-1
Down In A Southern Town......................mx 148221-2

15446-D (as by Claude Davis & Bob Nichols)
....(Apr 11, 1929)
Underneath The Southern Moon...............mx 148249-1
Meet Me Tonight In Dreamland................mx 148250-2

15740-D (as by Claude Davis Trio)
....(Nov 2, 1931)
Standing by The Highway......................mx 152005-1
I Don't Want Your Gold Or Silver.............mx 152006-1

THE DEAL FAMILY
15147-D...(Mar 31, 1927)
Everybody Will Be Happy Over There........mx 143832-2
I'm A Rolling.....................................mx 143837-1

15176-D...(Mar 31, 1927)
Working And Singing...........................mx 143833-2
Be A Daniel.......................................mx 143835-2

THE DEAL FAMILY

15191-D..(Mar 31, 1927)
A Wonderful Time...............................mx 143834-2
The Sinless Summerland......................mx 143836-1

15214-D..(Nov 5, 1927)
Beautiful Home Somewhere...................mx 145124-1
He's Coming Again.............................mx 145128-2

15248-D..(Nov 5, 1927)
Twill Be All Glory Over There................mx 145125-2
Joy Among The Angels........................mx 145129-2

15285-D..(Apr 14, 1928)
Jesus Paid It All..................................mx 146070-2
God Shall Wipe Our Tears Away.............mx 146071-2

15359-D..(Nov 5, 1927)
I'm On My Way To Glory......................mx 145127-2
Oh Come..................................……......mx 145126-2

15412-D..(Apr 19, 1929)
You Must Unload...............................mx 148365-2
Give Me Your Hand............................mx 148366-1

15451-D..(Apr 19, 1929)
The Glory Train..................….............mx 148367-2
Rocking On The Waves........................mx 148370-2

15670-D..(Apr 19, 1929)
The Home Coming Week......................mx 148368-1
Where Shall I Be................................mx 148369-2

DELMORE BROTHERS

15724-D..(Oct 28, 1931)
Got The Kansas City Blues....................mx 151976-1
Alabama Lullaby...............................mx 151977-1

THE DENSON QUARTET

15526-D..(Oct 29, 1928)
Christian Soldier................................mx 147331-2
I'm on My Journey Home.....................mx 147332-2

DIXIE STRING BAND

15273-D..(Nov 3, 1927)
Dixie Waltz.......................................mx 145095-2
Aldora Waltz.....................................mx 145096-2

DUNCAN SISTERS (Verna Lee & Lottie Jo)
15745-D..(Oct 26, 1931)
Dusty Roads.......................................mx 151949-1
See Sawyer Sisters 15745-D

EAST TEXAS SERENADERS
15229-D..(Dec 2, 1927)
Sweetest Flower..................................mx 145310-2
Combination Rag.................................mx 145311-2

GEORGE EDGIN'S CORN DODGERS With EARL WRIGHT & BROWN RICH
15754-D...(Mar 18, 1932)
My Ozark Mountain Home....................mx 152148-1
Corn Dodger No.1 Special....................mx 152153-1

ETOWAH QUARTET
15635-D...(Apr 18, 1928)
For Me...mx 146128-1
Who Is That......................................mx 146129-1

CLYDE EVANS BAND
15597-D..(Nov 4, 1929)
How I Got My Gal..............................mx 149365-2
All Gone Now....................................mx 149366-2

ROY EVANS
15252-D..(Apr 1928)
Weary Yodelin' Blues Part 1..................mx 146020-1
Weary Yodelin' Blues Part 2..................mx 146021-2

15272-D...(June 1928)
I Ain't Got Nobody And Nobody Cares For Me
....mx 146553-1
Dusky Stevedore.................................mx 146554-3

15687-D
Willie The Weeper................mx 146022 / Apr 11, 1928
See Overton Hatfield 15687-D

CLAY EVERHART & NORTH CAROLINA COOPER BOYS
15737-D...(Oct 27, 1931)
Standing By A Window........................mx 151950-1
The Rose With A Broken Stem..............mx 151952-1

JOSEPH F. FALCON

15275-D...(Apr 27, 1928)
The Waltz That Carried Me To My Grave (La Valce
Quii Ma Portin D Ma Fose).....................mx 146216-2
Lafayette (Allon A Luafette)....................mx 146217-2

15301-D (as by With Clemo Breaux)
....(Aug 27, 1928)
Fe Fe Ponchaux.................................mx 146904-1
Le Vieux Soulard Et Sa Femme (The Old Drunkard
And His Wife)....................................mx 146908-1

15325-D (as by With Clemo Breaux)
....(Aug 27, 1928)
Vieux Airs (Old Tunes).........................mx 146906-1
La Marche De La Noce (Wedding March)
....mx 146909-2

BOB FERGUSON
See Bob Miller

ELZIE FLOYD & LEO BOSWELL (See Leo Boswell)

15150-D...(Mar 26, 1927)
She's Only A Bird In A Gilded Cage..........mx 143763-2
Nellie Dare..mx 143768-2

15167-D...(Mar 26, 1927)
Lonesome Valley.................................mx 143766-1
The Two Orphans................................mx 143767-1

OSCAR FORD

15437-D...(Apr 11, 1929)
Henry Ford's Model A...........................mx 148240-1
Married Life Blues................................mx 148241-2

15554-D...(Apr 17, 1930)
Me And my Gal...................................mx 150253-2
Riding In A Chevrolet Six.......................mx 150254-2

15599-D...(Apr 17, 1930)
Sweetest Girl in Town...........................mx 150255-2
The Farmer's Dream.............................mx 150256-2

15634-D...(Dec 5, 1930)
Race Between A Ford And Chevrolet.........mx 151047-2
Georgia Is My Home.............................mx 151048-1

OSCAR FORD

15673-D..(Dec 5, 1930)
The Girl I Love In Tennessee...................mx 151045-2
Little Nan...mx 151046-2

JOE FOSS & His HUNGRY SAND LAPPERS
15268-D..(Apr 12, 1928)
Wee Dog Waltz...................................mx 146030-2
Oh! How She Lied..............................mx 146031-1

FREEMAN & ASHCRAFT
15442-D...(Apr 15, 1929)
I'll Still Write Your Name In The Sand
....mx 148301-2
Alabama Rag......................................mx 148302-1

GANUS BROTHERS
15331-D..(Oct 27, 1928)
Sometime We'll Say Goodbye..................mx 147316-2
Wondrous Love..................................mx 147317-2

15390-D **(as by Ganus Brothers Quartet)**
....(Oct 27, 1928)
Have A Sunny Smile............................mx 147314-2
Rejoice In God....................................mx 147315-1

GARLAND BROTHERS & GRINSTEAD
15679-D..(Oct 18, 1928)
Just Over The River.............................mx 147234-1
Beautiful..mx 147235-2

JOHNNIE GATES
15573-D..(June 2, 1930)
Saw Mill Blues No.1.............................mx 150541-2
Don't Leave Mother Alone......................mx 150542-1

15661-D **(as by Johnnie Gates The Saw Mill Yodeler)**
....(June 2, 1930)
Saw Mill Blues No.2............................mx 150543-2
The Little Pale Face Girl........................mx 150544-3

GATWOOD SQUARE DANCE BAND
15363-D...(Dec 15, 1928)
Third Party..mx 147646-2
Shear The Sheep Bobbie........................mx 147647-1

THE GEORGIA ORGAN GRINDERS
(McMichen, Layne, Stokes & Norris)
15394-D..(Apr 9, 1929)
Back Up And Push...............................mx 148222-2
Smoke Behind The Clouds.....................mx 148223-2

15415-D...(Apr 10, 1929)
Skip To My Lou My Darling....................mx 148231-2
Charming Betsy...................................mx 148232-2

15445-D...(Apr 10, 1929)
Four Thousand Years Ago......................mx 148227-2
Georgia Man..mx 148228-2

SHORTY GODWIN
15411-D...(Apr 12, 1929)
Jimbo Jambo Land................................mx 148262-2
Turnip Greens.....................................mx 148263-2

GORDON COUNTY QUARTET
15713-D...(Apr 18, 1930)
Walking In The Kings Highway................mx 150281-2
Beyond The Clouds Is Light...................mx 150282-2

FRED & GERTRUDE GOSSETT
15596-D...(Apr 16, 1930)
All The Good Times Are Passed And Gone
....mx 150232-1
Go Bury Me..mx 150233-1

THE GRADY FAMILY
15633-D...(Dec 6, 1930)
Gold Diggers......................................mx 151073-1
Carolina's Best....................................mx 151075-1

GRANT BROTHERS & THEIR MUSIC
15322-D...(Oct 15, 1928)
When A Man Is Married........................mx 147178-1
Tell It To Me......................................mx 147180-2

15460-D...(Oct 15, 1928)
Goodbye My Honey - I'm Gone...............mx 147179-1
Johnson Boy.......................................mx 147181-2

CLARENCE GREENE
15311-D **(as by Clarence Green)**............(Nov 5, 1927)
On The Banks Of The Ohio....................mx 145122-2
Fond Affection....................................mx 145123-2

CLARENCE GREENE

15461-D **(as by Clarence Green)**...............(Oct 15, 1928)
Johnson City Blues.............................mx 147190-2
Ninety Nine Years In Jail......................mx 147191-1

15680-D **(as by Clarence Green & Wise Brothers)**
....(Oct 15, 1928)
Pride Of The Ball..............................mx 147188-2
Kitty Waltz.....................................mx 147189-1

GREENSBORO BOYS QUARTET

15507-D..(Oct 16, 1928)
Sing Me A Song Of The Sunny South.........mx 147198-1
Sweet Little Girl of Mine......................mx 147199-2

MR. & MRS. R. N. GRISHAM

15177-D..(Apr 13, 1927)
Reaching To You...............................mx 143965-1
We'll Be At Home Again......................mx 143966-2

15255-D **(as by Mr. & Mrs. Grisham & Daughter)**
....(Oct 24, 1927)
Angels Tell My Mother I'll Be There...........mx 14004-2
Tis Wonderful..................................mx 145005-1

15305-D **(as by Mr. & Mrs. Grisham & Daughter / Mr. & Mrs. R.N. Grisham)**
....(Apr 26, 1928)
Just Beyond The Gates.........................mx 146199-1
I'll Be A Friend To Jesus......................mx 146202-2

15379-D **(as by Mr. & Mrs. Grisham & Daughter / Mr. & Mrs. R.N. Grisham**
....(Apr 26, 1928)
We're Drifting On..............................mx 146200-2
The Heart That Was Broken For Me...........mx 146201-2

E.E. HACK STRING BAND

15418-D..(Apr 17, 1929)
Too Tight Rag..................................mx 148336-2
West Kentucky Limited........................mx 148337-2

15466-D..(Apr 17, 1929)
Black Lake Waltz..............................mx 148334-2
Waltz Of Dreams...............................mx 148335-2

SID HAMPTON (The Yodelin' Man From Dixie Land)

15555-D..(May 3, 1930)
Swanee Sweetheart................................mx 150502-2
Kicking Mule..mx 150503-1

15583-D..(May 3, 1930)
The Hills Of Tennessee..........................mx 150432-2
I'll Be With You Mother.........................mx 150500-2

THE HAPPY FOUR

15164-D..(Apr 6, 1927)
He Knows How....................................mx 143924-2
(see 15164-D Copperhill Male Quartet)

15225-D..(Nov 11, 1927)
Climbing Up The Golden Stairs...............mx 145221-2
Come And Dine...................................mx 145220-2

HAPPY JACK

15720-D..(Oct 27, 1931)
I'm Only Suggesting This.......................mx 151960-1
The Wooden Wedding..........................mx 151961-1

ERNEST HARE

15742-D..(Feb 3, 1932)
Them Good Old Times (Are Comin' Back Again)
....mx 152100-1
Gene The Fighting Marine.....................mx 152101-1

RICHARD HAROLD

15426-D..(Oct 16, 1928)
Sweet Bird..mx 147204-1
Mary Dear..mx 147205-1

15586-D..(Oct 16, 1928)
The Battleship Maine...........................mx 147202-2
The Fisher's Maid................................mx 147203-1

GEORGE E. HARRIS

15543-D..(Feb 12, 1930)
That's The Blue Heaven For Me..............mx 149814-2
Since I've Grown So Used To You...........mx 149815-2

ROY HARVEY
(See Earl Shirkey & *Roy Harper*)
(Pseudonym for *Roy Harvey*)

15155-D (as by Roy Harvey & Posey Rorer)
....(May 12, 1927)
When The Bees Are In The Hive...............mx 144131-1
Daisies Won't Tell................................mx 144139 -2

15174-D (as by Roy Harvey North Carolina Ramblers)
The Wreck Of Virginian No. 3
.....................................mx 144520-2 / July 26, 1927
The Brave Engineer............mx 142640-2 / Sept 17, 1926

15514-D (as by Roy Harvey & Leonard Copeland)
....(Oct 22, 1929)
Just Pickin'...mx 149216-2
Beckley Rag..mx 149217-2

15582-D (as by Roy Harvey & Leonard Copeland)
....(Oct 22, 1929)
Underneath The Sugar Moon....................mx 149218-2
Lonesome Weary Blues..........................mx 149219-2

15609-D (as by Roy Harvey)...................(Sept 9, 1930)
Just Goodbye I Am Going Home...............mx 150781-2
The Lilly Reunion................................mx 150782-1

15637-D (as by Roy Harvey & Leonard Copeland)
....(Apr 22, 1930)
Greasy Wagon....................................mx 150337-2
Mother's Waltz...................................mx 150338-2

15714-D (as by Roy Harvey & Posey Rorer)
....(May 11, 1927)
Dark Eyes..mx 144123-1
Willie, Poor Boy..................................mx 144128-2

OVERTON HATFIELD (pseudonym for Gene Autry)
15687-D
A Gangster's Warning.........mx 151321-1 / Feb 17, 1931

MINER HAWKINS
15067-D..(Mar 9, 1926)
A Coal Miner's Dream..........................mx 141779-2
Song Of The Sea.................................mx 141780-2

TED HAWKINS MOUNTAINEERS
15752-D...(Nov 2, 1931)
Roamin' Jack......................................mx 152001-1
When The Lillies Bloom Again (In Old Kentucky)
....mx 152002-1

DEWEY HAYES (The Carolina Troubadour)
15753-D...(Oct 22, 1931)
Bring Back The One I Love.....................mx 151902-1
Cowboy's Prayer ....mx 151903-1

ED HELTON SINGERS
15327-D...(Oct 18, 1928)
A Storm On The Sea (The Sinking Of The Steamship
Vestris)...................................mx 147232-1
My Old Cottage Home.........................mx 147233-2

HENDERSONVILLE DOUBLE QUARTET
15443-D...(Apr 16, 1929)
Onward Ye Soldiers............................mx 148313-2
I Want My Life To Testify......................mx 148314-2

LEN & JOE HIGGINS
15243-D...(Feb 24, 1928)
Kentucky Wedding Chimes....................mx 145683-2
Medley Of Old Southern Melodies............mx 145684-3

15354-D...(Oct 17, 1928)
The Old White Mule............................mx 147123-3
Slippery Elm Tree...............................mx 147124-1

THE HOME TOWN BOYS
15736-D...(Oct 26, 1931)
Still Write Your Name In The Sand............mx 151944-1
Still Got 99..mx 151945-1

15762-D...(Oct 26, 1931)
Raccoon On A Rail..............................mx 151942-1
Home Town Rag................................mx 151943-1

DAN HORNSBY
15276-D **(as by Dan Hornsby Trio)**......(Apr 20, 1928)
On Mobile Bay..................................mx 146165-2
I Want A Girl (Just Like The Girl That Married Dear
Old Dad)..mx 146166-2

15321-D...(Oct 23, 1928)
The Story Of C.S. Carnes......................mx 147270-2
The Shelby Disaster............................mx 147271-2

DAN HORNSBY

15381-D (as by Dan Hornsby Trio).........(Nov 1, 1928)
She Was Bred In Old Kentucky.................mx 147373-2
Can't Yo' Heah Me Callin' Caroline...........mx 147374-2

15444-D (as by Dan Hornsby Novelty Quartet)
....(Apr 14, 1929)
Take Me Out To The Ball Game................mx 148277-1
Hinky Dinky Dee.................................mx 148278-2

15578-D (as by Dan Hornsby).................(Nov 1, 1928)
Just A Baby's Prayer At Twilight..............mx 147377-1
I'm Sorry I Made You Cry......................mx 147378-1

15628-D (as by Dan Hornsby)...............(Dec 12, 1930)
History In A Few Words........................mx 151133-1
The Lunatic's Lullaby..........................mx 151134-2

15769-D (as by Dan Hornsby Trio / Dan Hornsby Novelty Orchestra)
Dear Old Girl...................mx 145168-1 / Nov 8, 1927
All Alone......................mx 148325-2 / Apr 17, 1929

15771-D (as by Dan Hornsby & His Lion's Den Trio)
....(Nov 3, 1931)
A Sailor's Sweetheart..........................mx 152016-1
Three Blind Mice...............................mx 152017-1

JACK JACKSON

15497-D...(Oct 21, 1929)
In Our Little Home Sweet Home................mx 149206-2
I'm Just A Black Sheep.........................mx 149207-2

15662-D...(Oct 21, 1929)
Flat Tire Blues.................................mx 149202-2
My Alabama Home..............................mx 149203-1

AUNT MOLLY JACKSON

15731-D...(Dec 10, 1931)
Kentucky Miner's Wife Part 1(Ragged Hungry Blues)
....mx 150240-1
Kentucky Miner's Wife Part 2..................mx 150241-1

JAMES JOHNSON

15453-D...(Oct 22, 1928)
Put On Your Old Grey Bonnet..................mx 147250-1
Papa Please Buy Me An Airship................mx 147251-2

ROY JONES

15428-D..(Apr 12, 1928)
Southern Yodel Blues............................mx 146036-2
Farmer John's Yodel.............................mx 146037-2

SAM JONES
See Stovepipe #1 – 15011-D

THE KENTUCKY GIRLS

15364-D..(Dec 6, 1928)
Old And Only In The Way......................mx 147583-2
Sweet Golden Daisies............................mx 147584-1

PIERRE LA DIEU

15278-D..(July 3, 1928)
The Shanty Man's Life..........................mx 146619-2
Driving Saw Logs On The Plover..............mx 146620-3

LEAKE COUNTY REVELERS

15149-D..(Apr 13, 1927)
Johnson Gal...mx 143967-2
Leather Breeches...................................mx 143968-2

15189-D..(Apr 13, 1927)
Good Night Waltz.................................mx 143970-1
Wednesday Night Waltz.........................mx 143969-1

15205-D..(Oct 25, 1927)
The Old Hat...mx 145016-2
Monkey In The Dog Cart........................mx 145017-2

15227-D..(Oct 25, 1927)
My Bonnie Lies Over The Ocean..............mx 145013-1
In The Good Old Summertime.................mx 145014-2

15264-D..(Apr 27, 1928)
Make Me A Bed On The Floor.................mx 146210-2
Merry Widow Waltz..............................mx 146211-2

15292-D..(Apr 27, 1928)
They Go Simply Wild Over Me................mx 146213-2
Put Me In My Little Bed.........................mx 146214-2

15318-D..(Apr 27, 1928)
Crow Black Chicken..............................mx 146209-3
Been To The East, Been To The West.........mx 146208-2

DAN HORNSBY

15381-D (as by Dan Hornsby Trio).........(Nov 1, 1928)
She Was Bred In Old Kentucky................mx 147373-2
Can't Yo' Heah Me Callin' Caroline..........mx 147374-2

15444-D (as by Dan Hornsby Novelty Quartet)
....(Apr 14, 1929)
Take Me Out To The Ball Game...............mx 148277-1
Hinky Dinky Dee...............................mx 148278-2

15578-D (as by Dan Hornsby)................(Nov 1, 1928)
Just A Baby's Prayer At Twilight..............mx 147377-1
I'm Sorry I Made You Cry......................mx 147378-1

15628-D (as by Dan Hornsby)..............(Dec 12, 1930)
History In A Few Words........................mx 151133-1
The Lunatic's Lullaby..........................mx 151134-2

15769-D (as by Dan Hornsby Trio / Dan Hornsby Novelty Orchestra)
Dear Old Girl...................mx 145168-1 / Nov 8, 1927
All Alone.....................mx 148325-2 / Apr 17, 1929

15771-D (as by Dan Hornsby & His Lion's Den Trio)
....(Nov 3, 1931)
A Sailor's Sweetheart..........................mx 152016-1
Three Blind Mice...............................mx 152017-1

JACK JACKSON

15497-D...(Oct 21, 1929)
In Our Little Home Sweet Home...............mx 149206-2
I'm Just A Black Sheep........................mx 149207-2

15662-D...(Oct 21, 1929)
Flat Tire Blues..................................mx 149202-2
My Alabama Home............................mx 149203-1

AUNT MOLLY JACKSON

15731-D...(Dec 10, 1931)
Kentucky Miner's Wife Part 1(Ragged Hungry Blues)
....mx 150240-1
Kentucky Miner's Wife Part 2..................mx 150241-1

JAMES JOHNSON

15453-D...(Oct 22, 1928)
Put On Your Old Grey Bonnet..................mx 147250-1
Papa Please Buy Me An Airship...............mx 147251-2

ROY JONES
15428-D..(Apr 12, 1928)
Southern Yodel Blues...........................mx 146036-2
Farmer John's Yodel............................mx 146037-2

SAM JONES
See Stovepipe #1 – 15011-D

THE KENTUCKY GIRLS
15364-D..(Dec 6, 1928)
Old And Only In The Way.....................mx 147583-2
Sweet Golden Daisies...........................mx 147584-1

PIERRE LA DIEU
15278-D..(July 3, 1928)
The Shanty Man's Life..........................mx 146619-2
Driving Saw Logs On The Plover..............mx 146620-3

LEAKE COUNTY REVELERS
15149-D..(Apr 13, 1927)
Johnson Gal......................................mx 143967-2
Leather Breeches................................mx 143968-2

15189-D..(Apr 13, 1927)
Good Night Waltz...............................mx 143970-1
Wednesday Night Waltz........................mx 143969-1

15205-D..(Oct 25, 1927)
The Old Hat......................................mx 145016-2
Monkey In The Dog Cart.......................mx 145017-2

15227-D..(Oct 25, 1927)
My Bonnie Lies Over The Ocean..............mx 145013-1
In The Good Old Summertime.................mx 145014-2

15264-D..(Apr 27, 1928)
Make Me A Bed On The Floor.................mx 146210-2
Merry Widow Waltz............................mx 146211-2

15292-D..(Apr 27, 1928)
They Go Simply Wild Over Me................mx 146213-2
Put Me In My Little Bed........................mx 146214-2

15318-D..(Apr 27, 1928)
Crow Black Chicken............................mx 146209-3
Been To The East, Been To The West.........mx 146208-2

LEAKE COUNTY REVELERS

15353-D..(Dec 13, 1928)
Julia Waltz...mx 147629-1
Rocking Yodel....................................mx 147626-2

15380-D
Bring Me A Bottle..............mx 147624-2 / Dec 12, 1928
Molly Put The Kettle On
....................................mx 147631-2 / Dec 13, 1928

15409-D..(Apr 16, 1929)
Georgia Camp Meeting..........................mx 148319-2
I'm Gwine Back To Dixie.......................mx 148320-2

15427-D..(Apr 16, 1929)
Memories Waltz....................................mx 148315-2
Where The Sil'vry Colorado Wends Its Way
....mx 148317-1

15441-D..(Apr 16, 1929)
Dry Town Blues...................................mx 148321-2
Good Fellow..mx 148323-2

15470-D..(Apr 16, 1929)
Saturday Night Breakdown......................mx 148322-2
Uncle Ned..mx 148324-2

15501-D..(Dec 10, 1929)
Sweet Rose Of Heaven..........................mx 149586-2
Beautiful Bells......................................mx 149587-2

15520-D..(Dec 10, 1929)
Leake County Blues..............................mx 149582-2
Lonesome Blues...................................mx 149583-1

15569-D..(Dec 10, 1929)
Mississippi Moon Waltz.........................mx 149588-2
Courtin' Days Waltz..............................mx 149589-2

15625-D..(Dec 13, 1928)
Birds In The Brook...............................mx 147625-2
Magnolia Waltz....................................mx 147628-2

15648-D..(Dec 18, 1930)
When It's Springtime In The Rockies.........mx 151121-1
Jungle Waltz..mx 151125-2

39

LEAKE COUNTY REVELERS

15668-D..(Dec 18, 1930)
Thirty First Street Blues.........................mx 151119-2
Mississippi Breakdown..........................mx 151123-2

15691-D..(Dec 18, 1930)
Picture No Artist Can Paint.....................mx 151120-2
Texas Fair..mx 151122-2

15767-D
Memories........................mx 147627-2 / Dec 13, 1928
Lazy Kate......................mx 151124-1 / Dec 18, 1930

15776-D..(Oct 25, 1927)
My Wild Irish Rose..............................mx 145012-2
Listen To The Mocking Bird...................mx 145015-2

MALCOLM LEGETTE

15424-D..(Oct 29, 1928)
Life On An Ocean Wave.......................mx 147327-2
Song Of The Tramp.............................mx 147328-1

LUBBOCK TEXAS QUARTET

15510-D...(Dec 6, 1929)
Turn Away...mx 149554-1
O Mother How We Miss You..................mx 149555-2

BASCOM LUNSFORD

15595-D..(Apr 15, 1930)
Speaking The Truth.............................mx 150228-2
A Stump Speech In The 10th District..........mx 150229-1

FRANK LUTHER
See Carson Robison

MACON QUARTET

15211-D...(Mar 28, 1927)
Uncle Joe...mx 143787-1
Yodel..mx 143788-2

JACK MAHONEY

15685-D..(June 15, 1931)
The Convict And The Bird.....................mx 151608-2
The Hobo And The Pie.........................mx 151609-1

15712-D..(June 15, 1931)
The Convict's Return............................mx 151684-1
Woodman Spare That Tree.....................mx 151685-1

JACK MAJOR
15362-D..(July 7, 1927)
Silver Moon..mx 144434-3
My Kentucky Mountain Sweetheart...........mx 144435-3

MARTIN MELODY BOYS
15413-D...(Apr 16, 1929)
An Old Sweetheart Of Mine....................mx 148310-2
The Donald Rag..................................mx 148311-1

FRANKIE MARVIN
15474-D **(as by The Marvin Family / Frankie Marvin)**
Life On The Ocean Wave
....mx 148605-2 / May 21, 1929
Yodeling Them Blues Away
....mx 148703-2 / June 14, 1929

15518-D **(as by Frankie Marvin)**..........(Sept 27, 1929)
Dust Pan Blues....................................mx 149070-2
Miss Moonshine..................................mx 149071-3

15568-D **(as by Frankie Marvin)**..........(Mar 18, 1930)
Oh, For The Wild And Woolly West..........mx 150090-3
Livin' in The Mountains........................mx 150091-2

JOHNNY MARVIN
15750-D..(Mar 2, 1932)
Seven Come Eleven ....mx 152112-1
Yodelin' My Way To Heaven..................mx 152114-1

MASSANUTTEN MILITARY ACADEMY QUARTET
15751-D...(Mar 28, 1932)
Drink To Me Only With Thine Eyes...........mx 152166-?
Nancy Lee...mx 152165-?

JACK MATHIS
15344-D..(Dec 3, 1928)
Your Mother Still Prays For You...............mx 147554-2
When The Roses Come Again..................mx 147555-2

15450-D..(Dec 9, 1928)
Charming Bessie Lee............................mx 147620-1
Annie Dear I'm Called Away...................mx 147621-1

McCARTT BROTHERS & PATTERSON
15454-D...(Oct 18, 1928)
Green Valley Waltz..............................mx 147242-2
Over The Sea Waltz.............................mx 147243-2

ED & GRACE McCONNELL

15291-D..(Apr 18, 1928)
I Want To Be Like Jesus........................mx 146124-2
My Loving Brother (Rock Of Ages)...........mx 146125-2

15780-D...(Apr 4, 1927)
Walking In The Light............................mx 143894-1
Leaving Smiles...................................mx 143895-3

EARL McCOY

15499-D (as by Earl McCoy & Jessie Brock)
Cotton Mill Girl..................mx 149393-1 / Nov 5, 1929
Are You Tired Of Me Darling
............................mx 149394-1 / Nov 6, 1929

15604-D (as by Earl McCoy & Jessie Brock)
....(Nov 6, 1929)
If I Could Hear My Mother Pray Again.......mx 149395-2
Off To War..mx 149396-2

15622-D (as by Earl McCoy, Alfred Meng & Clem Garner)
....(Apr 23, 1930)
John Henry The Steel Drivin' Man.............mx 150370-2
Forty Per Cent...................................mx 150371-1

WILLIAM McCOY

15269-D..(Dec 1927)
Train Imitations And Fox Chase................mx 145335-1
Mama Blues.......................................mx 145334-2

FRANK & JAMES McCRAVY

15544-D...(Mar 28, 1930)
The Great Judgment Morning...................mx 150146-3
The Dollar And The Devil......................mx 150147-2

15617-D...(Mar 28, 1930)
The Better Home................................mx 150145-1
No More Dying..................................mx 150148-1

15764-D...(Apr 2, 1930)
I Love You In The Same Old Way (Darling Sue)
....mx 150163-3
Don't Forget To Drop A Line To Mother.....mx 150164-1

BOB McGIMSEY
See Bob Brookes

JACK MAJOR
15362-D...(July 7, 1927)
Silver Moon...mx 144434-3
My Kentucky Mountain Sweetheart...........mx 144435-3

MARTIN MELODY BOYS
15413-D...(Apr 16, 1929)
An Old Sweetheart Of Mine.....................mx 148310-2
The Donald Rag....................................mx 148311-1

FRANKIE MARVIN
15474-D (as by The Marvin Family / Frankie Marvin)
Life On The Ocean Wave
......................................mx 148605-2 / May 21, 1929
Yodeling Them Blues Away
......................................mx 148703-2 / June 14, 1929

15518-D **(as by Frankie Marvin)**..........(Sept 27, 1929)
Dust Pan Blues....................................mx 149070-2
Miss Moonshine..................................mx 149071-3

15568-D **(as by Frankie Marvin)**..........(Mar 18, 1930)
Oh, For The Wild And Woolly West.........mx 150090-3
Livin' in The Mountains........................mx 150091-2

JOHNNY MARVIN
15750-D...(Mar 2, 1932)
Seven Come Eleven ....mx 152112-1
Yodelin' My Way To Heaven..................mx 152114-1

MASSANUTTEN MILITARY ACADEMY QUARTET
15751-D...(Mar 28, 1932)
Drink To Me Only With Thine Eyes..........mx 152166-?
Nancy Lee..mx 152165-?

JACK MATHIS
15344-D...(Dec 3, 1928)
Your Mother Still Prays For You..............mx 147554-2
When The Roses Come Again.................mx 147555-2

15450-D...(Dec 9, 1928)
Charming Bessie Lee............................mx 147620-1
Annie Dear I'm Called Away...................mx 147621-1

McCARTT BROTHERS & PATTERSON
15454-D...(Oct 18, 1928)
Green Valley Waltz..............................mx 147242-2
Over The Sea Waltz.............................mx 147243-2

ED & GRACE McCONNELL

15291-D..(Apr 18, 1928)
I Want To Be Like Jesus.........................mx 146124-2
My Loving Brother (Rock Of Ages)...........mx 146125-2

15780-D..(Apr 4, 1927)
Walking In The Light............................mx 143894-1
Leaving Smiles...................................mx 143895-3

EARL McCOY

15499-D (as by Earl McCoy & Jessie Brock)
Cotton Mill Girl..................mx 149393-1 / Nov 5, 1929
Are You Tired Of Me Darling
....mx 149394-1 / Nov 6, 1929

15604-D (as by Earl McCoy & Jessie Brock)
....(Nov 6, 1929)
If I Could Hear My Mother Pray Again.......mx 149395-2
Off To War...mx 149396-2

15622-D (as by Earl McCoy, Alfred Meng & Clem Garner)
....(Apr 23, 1930)
John Henry The Steel Drivin' Man.............mx 150370-2
Forty Per Cent....................................mx 150371-1

WILLIAM McCOY

15269-D..(Dec 1927)
Train Imitations And Fox Chase................mx 145335-1
Mama Blues..mx 145334-2

FRANK & JAMES McCRAVY

15544-D..(Mar 28, 1930)
The Great Judgment Morning...................mx 150146-3
The Dollar And The Devil.......................mx 150147-2

15617-D..(Mar 28, 1930)
The Better Home.................................mx 150145-1
No More Dying...................................mx 150148-1

15764-D..(Apr 2, 1930)
I Love You In The Same Old Way (Darling Sue)
....mx 150163-3
Don't Forget To Drop A Line To Mother.....mx 150164-1

BOB McGIMSEY
See Bob Brookes

CLAYTON McMICHEN (pseudonym Bob Nichols)

15095-D (as by Riley Puckett & Bob Nichols)
....(Apr 22, 1926)
I'm Drifting Back To Dreamland...............mx 142084-1
My Carolina Home..............................mx 142085-1

15111-D (as by McMichen's Melody Men)
....(Nov 4, 1926)
Let Me Call You Sweetheart....................mx 143056-2
Sweet Bunch Of Daisies.........................mx 143057-1

15114-D (as by Bob Nichols & Riley Puckett)
....(Nov 6, 1926)
My Isle Of Golden Dreams......................mx 143101-2
Don't You Remember That Time...............mx 143100-1

15130-D (as by McMichen's Melody Men)
....(Nov 6, 1926)
House Of David Blues...........................mx 143090-1
Down Yonder.....................................mx 143091-2

15136-D (as by McMichen's Melody Men)
....(Nov 6, 1926)
Underneath The Mellow Moon.................mx 143099-1
Ring Waltz..mx 143098-2

15140-D (as by Clayton McMichen, Riley Puckett, Gid Tanner, Fate Norris, Bob Nichols & Bert Layne)
....(Apr 1, 1927)
Fiddler's Convention In Georgia Part 1
....mx 143848-1
Fiddler's Convention In Georgia Part 2
....mx 143849-2

15161-D (as by Bob Nichols & Riley Puckett)
....(Mar 30, 1927)
Till We Meet Again..............................mx 143814-2
I'm Forever Blowing Bubbles..................mx 143815-2

15190-D...(Mar 26, 1927)
St. Louis Blues...................................mx 143769-1
Fiddlin' Medley (Old Time Fiddlers Medley)
....mx 143770-1

CLAYTON McMICHEN (pseudonym Bob Nichols)

15198-D (as by Bob Nichols & Riley Puckett)
Let The Rest Of The World Go By
...................................mx 143813-1 / Mar 30, 1927
That Old Irish Mother Of mine
.....................................mx 143854-2 / Apr 1, 1927

15201-D (as by Clayton McMichen, Riley Puckett, Gid Tanner, Lowe Stokes, Fate Norris, Bob Nichols & Bill Brown)
....(Nov 1, 1927)
A Corn Licker Still In Georgia Part 1..........mx 145066-3
A Corn Licker Still In Georgia Part 2..........mx 145067-2

15202-D (as by McMichen's Melody Men)
....(Nov 4, 1927)
Aloha Oe (Farewell To Thee)...................mx 145099-1
The Missouri Waltz..............................mx 145100-2

15216-D (as by Bob Nichols & Riley Puckett)
My Blue Ridge Mountain Queen
......................................mx 145068-1 / Nov 1, 1927
In The Shade Of The Old Apple Tree
....................................mx 145090-3 / Nov 3, 1927

15224-D (as by McMichen's Melody Men)
My Carolina Home................mx 145077 / Nov 2, 1927
Fifty Tears Ago.....................mx 145102 / Nov 4, 1927

15232-D (as by Riley Puckett & Clayton McMichen)
....(Apr 2, 1927)
Cindy...mx 143867-2
Little Brown Jug.................................mx 143868-2

15247-D (as by McMichen's Melody Men)
....(Nov 1, 1927)
When You And I Were Young, Maggie.......mx 145059-1
Silver Threads Among The Gold...............mx 145060-1

15253-D (as by Clayton McMichen & Dan Hornsby)
....(Apr 12, 1928)
The Original Arkansas Traveler Part 1
....mx 146038-1 / Apr 1928
The Original Arkansas Traveler Part 2
....mx 146039-3 / Apr 1928

CLAYTON McMICHEN (pseudonym Bob Nichols)

15258-D (as by Clayton McMichen, Riley Puckett, Gid Tanner, Lowe Stokes, Fate Norris, Bob Nichols & Bill Brown)
....(Apr 12, 1928)
Corn Licker Still In Georgia Part 3.............mx 146032-1
Corn Licker Still In Georgia Part 4.............mx 146033-2

15288-D (as by McMichen's Melody Men with Riley Puckett)
....(Apr 14, 1928)
Where The River Shannon Flows..............mx 146076-2
Home Sweet Home..............................mx 146077-1

15295-D (as by Riley Puckett & Clayton McMichen)
....(Apr 14, 1928)
Slim Gal..mx 146078-2
Old Molly Hare..................................mx 146079-2

15304-D (as by Bob Nichols & Riley Puckett)
Trail Of The Lonesome Pine
..................................mx 145083-2 / Nov 2, 1927
Neath The Old Apple Tree
..................................mx 146080-1 / Apr 14, 1928

15310-D (as by McMichen's Melody Men)
Ain't She Sweet?.....................mx 145061-2 / Nov 1, 1927
Darling Nellie Gray.............mx 145101-2 / Nov 4, 1927

15332-D (as by Fate Norris, Gid Tanner, Hugh Cross, Lowe Stokes, Clayton McMichen & K.D. Malone)
....(Oct 24, 1928)
A Day At The County Fair Part 1...............mx 147278-2
A Day At The County Fair Part 2...............mx 147279-3

15333-D (as by McMichen – Layne String Orchestra)
....(Oct 26, 1928)
The Blind Child's Prayer Part 1.................mx 147308-2
The Blind Child's Prayer Part 2...............mx 147309-3

15340-D (as by McMichen's Melody Men)
....(Oct 24, 1928)
Wabash Blues....................................mx 147284-2
Lonesome Mama Blues.........................mx 147285-2

CLAYTON McMICHEN (pseudonym Bob Nichols)

15350-D (as by Bob Nichols & Riley Puckett)
....(Apr 11, 1928)
Dear Old Dixieland..............................mx 146025-3
When The Maple Leaves Are Falling..........mx 146024-2

15356-D (as by McMichen – Layne String Orchestra)
Down On The Ozark Trail
...................................mx 147274-2 / Oct 24, 1928
Daisies Won't Tell..............mx 147310-2 / Oct 26, 1928

15358-D (as by Riley Puckett & Clayton McMichen)
....(Oct 26, 1928)
Bill Johnson..mx 147297-2
Paddy Won't You Drink Some Cider.........mx 147299-1

15366-D (as by Clayton McMichen, Riley Puckett, Gid Tanner, Lowe Stokes & Fate Norris)
....(Oct 24, 1928)
Corn Licker Still In Georgia Part 5.............mx 147275-3
Corn Licker Still In Georgia Part 6.............mx 147276-3

15391-D (as by McMichen's Melody Men)
When You're Far From The Ones Who Love You
...................................mx 147277-2 / Oct 24, 1928
Sailing On The Bay Of Tripoli
...................................mx 147286-2 / Oct 25, 1928

15432-D (as by Clayton McMichen, Riley Puckett, Gid Tanner, Lowe Stokes, Fate Norris & Tom Dorsey)
....(Apr 12, 1929)
Corn Licker Still In Georgia Part 7.............mx 148266-3
Corn Licker Still In Georgia Part 8.............mx 148267-3

15464-D (as by McMichen – Layne String Orchestra)
....(Oct 23, 1928)
Little Blue Ridge Girl...........................mx 147261-1
The Dying Hobo.................................mx 147262-3

15480-D (as by Bob Nichols & Hugh Cross)
....(Nov 1, 1929)
Corrine Corrina...................................mx 149334-2
I Left My Gal In The Mountains...............mx 149335-2

CLAYTON McMICHEN (pseudonym Bob Nichols)

15482-D (as by Hugh Cross, Clayton McMichen, Riley Puckett, Gid Tanner, Fate Norris & Lowe Stokes)
....(Nov 2, 1929)
Kickapoo Medicine Show Part 1...............mx 149338-3
Kickapoo Medicine Show Part 2...............mx 149339-3

15503-D (as by Clayton McMichen, Riley Puckett, Gid Tanner, Lowe Stokes, Fate Norris, Bert Layne, Uncle Fuzz & Tom Dorsey)
....(Nov 2, 1929)
A Night In A Blind Tiger Part 1.................mx 140340-1
A Night In A Blind Tiger Part 2.................mx 149341-1

15521-D (as by Clayton McMichen & Riley Puckett)
....(Oct 29, 1929)
McMichen's Reel...............................mx 149289-2
Rye Straw......................................mx 149290-2

15531-D (as by Clayton McMichen, Riley Puckett, Gid Tanner, Lowe Stokes, Fate Norris & Tom Dorsey)
....(Nov 1, 1929)
Corn Licker Still In Georgia Part 9.............mx 149328-2
Corn Licker Still In Georgia Part 10............mx 149329-2

15540-D (as by McMichen's Melody Men)
....(Oct 31, 1929)
Honolulu moon.................................mx 149316-1
When Clouds Have Vanished...................mx 149317-2

15549-D (as by Clayton McMichen, Riley Puckett, Gid Tanner, Lowe Stokes, Bert Layne, Fate Norris, Oscar Ford & Tom Dorsey)
....(Apr 17, 1930)
Taking The Census Part 1.....................mx 150271-3
Taking The Census Part 2.....................mx 150272-1

15556-D (as by Bob Nichols & Hugh Cross)
In The Hills Of Old Virginia
....mx 150237-2 / Apr 16, 1930
Smoky Mountain Home.......mx 150343-2 / Apr 22, 1930

15590-D (as by Bob Nichols)..................(Apr 15, 1930)
The Killing Of Tom Slaughter..................mx 150218-3
The Grave In The Pines........................mx 150219-3

CLAYTON McMICHEN (pseudonym Bob Nichols)

15594-D (as by Clayton McMichen & Riley Puckett)
....(Apr 21, 1930)
Done Gone..mx 150327-2
Cumberland Valley Waltz.......................mx 150328-2

15598-D (as by Clayton McMichen, Riley Puckett, Gid Tanner, Lowe Stokes, Bert Layne, Oscar Ford & Tom Dorsey)
....(Apr 19, 1930)
Jeremiah Hopkins Store At Sand Mountain Part 1
....mx 150299-2
Jeremiah Hopkins Store At Sand Mountain Part 2
....mx 150300-2

15618-D (as by Clayton McMichen, Riley Puckett, Gid Tanner, Lowe Stokes, Fate Norris & Tom Dorsey)
....(Apr 21, 1930)
Corn Licker Still In Georgia Part 11............mx 150335-1
Corn Licker Still In Georgia Part 12............mx 150336-1

15632-D (as by Clayton McMichen, Riley Puckett, Lowe Stokes, Bert Layne & Tom Dorsey)
....(Dec 8, 1930)
Prohibition – Yes Or No Part 1..................mx 151098-3
Prohibition – Yes Or No Part 2..................mx 151099-1

15667-D (as by Clayton McMichen, Riley Puckett, Gid Tanner, Lowe Stokes, Bert Layne & Tom Dorsey)
....(Dec 8, 1930)
Fiddlers Convention Part 3......................mx 151100-3
Fiddlers Convention Part 4......................mx 151101-2

15698-D (as by Bob Nichols & Hugh Cross)
When I Lived In Arkansas
..................................mx 150236-1 / Apr 16, 1930
When It's Peach Picking Time in Georgia
..........................mx 150320-2 / Apr 21, 1930

15700-D (as by Clayton McMichen, Riley Puckett, Gid Tanner, Lowe Stokes & Fate Norris)
....(Nov 4, 1929)
A Bee Hunt On Hill For Sartin Creek Part 1
....mx 149369-3
A Bee Hunt On Hill For Sartin Creek Part 2
....mx 149370-1

CLAYTON McMICHEN (pseudonym Bob Nichols)

15703-D (as by Clayton McMichen, Riley Puckett, Gid Tanner, Lowe Stokes, Bert Layne & Tom Dorsey)
....(Dec 8, 1930)
Corn Licker Still In Georgia Part 13............mx 151102-1
Corn Licker Still In Georgia Part 12............mx 151103-3

15723-D (as by MicMichen's Georgia Wildcats with Slim Bryant)
....(Oct 26, 1931)
When The Bloom Is On The Sage..............mx 151932-1
Yum Yum Blues.................................mx 151933-1

15775-D (as by Clayton McMichen's Georgia Wildcats)
....(Oct 28, 1931)
Wild Cat Rag......................................mx 151966-1
Sweet Floreine...................................mx 151971-1

McMILLAN QUARTET

15194-D...(Apr 2, 1927)
Glory Is Coming................................mx 143863-2
No Stranger Yonder............................mx 143864-2

15681-D...(Apr 20, 1928)
I Love To Tell His Love........................mx 146157-1
Singing On The Journey Home................mx 146158-2

McVAY & JOHNSON

15370-D...(Oct 17, 1928)
Ain't Going To Lay My Armor Down
....mx 147224-1
I'll Be Ready When The Bridegroom Comes
....mx 147225-2

MELTON & WAGGONER

15423-D...(Oct 30, 1928)
In The Hills Of Old Kentucky (My Mountain Rose)
....mx 147337-2
Underneath The Cotton Moon..................mx 147338-2

BOB MILLER (pseudonym Bob Ferguson)

15297-D (as by Bob Ferguson)
....(Aug 17, 1928)
Eleven Cent Cotton Forty Cent Meat Part 1
....mx 146855-1
Eleven Cent Cotton Forty Cent Meat Part 2
....mx 146852-2

15433-D (as by Bob Ferguson & His Scalawaggers)
....(July 3, 1929)
Keep On Keepin' On............................mx 148779-2
Toodle Lolly Day................................mx 148780-1

15476-D (as by Bob Ferguson & His Scalawaggers)
....(Oct 21, 1929)
The Farmer's Letter To The President.........mx 149161-2
Dry Votin' Wet Drinkers........................mx 149162-2

15529-D (as by Bob Ferguson & His Scalawaggers)
....(July 22, 1929)
Golden Wings....................................mx 148832-1

Missouri Joe.....................................mx 148833-2

15553-D (as by Bob Ferguson & His Scalawaggers)
....(Apr 16, 1930)
They're Hanging Old Jonesy Tomorrow
....mx 150473-2
Prisoner's Letter To the Governor..............mx 150474-2

15558-D (as by Charlotte Miller & Bob Ferguson)
....(Apr 16, 1930)
Poker Alice......................................mx 150471-2
Dangerous Nan McGrew........................mx 150472-2

15616-D (as by Bob Ferguson & His Scalawaggers)
....(Jan 31, 1930)
Wild And Reckless Hobo........................mx 149947-2
Little Red Caboose..............................mx 149948-3

15657-D (as by Bob Ferguson & Charlotte Miller)
....(Mar 9, 1931)
Corn Pone And Pot Likker (Crumbled Or Drunked) Part 1
....mx 151409-3
Corn Pone And Pot Likker (Crumbled Or Drunked) Part 2
....mx 151410-3

BOB MILLER (pseudonym Bob Ferguson)
15664-D (as by Bob Ferguson & His Scalawaggers)
....(Feb 25, 1931)
1930 Drought......................................mx 151351-3
Bank Failures.....................................mx 151352-3

15677-D (as by Bob Ferguson)
The Strawberry Roan..........mx 151557-1 / May 20, 1931
See Cartwright Brothers 15677-D

15704-D **(as by Bob Ferguson)**............(July 15, 1931)
Clover Blossoms................................mx 151686-1
Anna May..mx 151687-1

15727-D (as by Bob Ferguson & His Scalawaggers / Uncle Bud & His Plow Boys) (Bob Miller)
....(Dec 1, 1931)
The Crime Of Harry Powers....................mx 151897-2
What Does The Deep Sea Say..................mx 365043-2

15732-D (as by Bob Ferguson & His Scalawaggers)
The Unmarked Grave..........mx 152039-1 / Dec 10, 1931
The Death Of Jack "Legs" Diamond
..............................mx 152050-4 / Dec 23, 1931

15735-D (as by Memphis Bob) (Bob Miller)
....(Dec 31, 1931)
Little Marian McLean...........................mx 152055-1
Beyond Prison Walls............................mx 152056-1

15739-D (as by Bob Ferguson & His Scalawaggers)
....(Jan 20, 1932)
"New" Twenty One Years.......................mx 152084-1
Fifty Years Repentin"...........................mx 152085-3

15759-D **(as by Bob Ferguson)**...............(June 9, 1932)
Charles A. Lindbergh Jr.........................mx 152197-1
There's A New Star Up in Heaven (Baby Lindy Up There)..mx 152198-1

15760-D **(as by The Shelby Singers)**........(May 4, 1932)
Nobody To Love................................mx 152184-1
The Voice In The Old Village Choir...........mx 152185-1

15761-D **(as by Bud Skidmore)**..............(May 4, 1932)
Behind The Big White House..................mx 152183-1
The Sad Song......................................mx 152186-1

BOB MILLER (pseudonym Bob Ferguson)
15782-D (as by Bob Ferguson / Columbia Band)
Crash Of The Akron..............mx 152386-2 / Apr 5, 1933
Anchors Aweigh...............mx 148748-? / June 21, 1929

MOATSVILLE STRING TICKLERS
15491-D...(Oct 22, 1929)
The West Virginia Hills.........................mx 149232-1
Moatsville Blues..................................mx 149233-2

REV. C.D. MONTGOMERY
15023-D..(Jan 1925)
Who Was Job #1..................................mx 140317-1
Who Was Job #2..................................mx 140318-1

BYRD MOORE & His HOT SHOTS
15496-D..(Oct 23, 1929)
Careless Love......................................mx 149242-1
Three Men Went A Hunting....................mx 149243-2

15536-D..(Oct 23, 1929)
Frankie Silvers....................................mx 149240-1
The Hills Of Tennessee.........................mx 149241-1

WALTER MORRIS
15079-D...(Apr 22, 1926)
Crazy Coon...mx 142082-1
Betsy Brown.......................................mx 142083-2

15101-D...(Apr 22, 1926)
Take Back Your Gold............................mx 142080-1
The Railroad Tramp..............................mx 142081-1

15115-D
Sweet Marie.......................mx 143067-1 / Nov 4, 1926
Lulu Walsh........................mx 143108-2 / Nov 6, 1926

15186-D...(Apr 6, 1927)
Mother's Face I Long To See...................mx 143911-1
In The Time Long Ago..........................mx 143912-2

MOUNT VERNON QUARTET
15245-D..(Apr 2, 1927)
The New Jerusalem Way.........................mx 143865-2
Tenting Tonight On The Old Camp Ground
....mx 143866-1

MURPHY BROTHERS HARP BAND
15646-D..(Dec 4, 1930)
Little Bunch Of Roses...........................mx 151022-2
Downfall Of Paris................................mx 151023-1

HINKY MYERS
15725-D..(Oct 30, 1931)
I'm Tying The Leaves...........................mx 151987-?
See Peggy Parker 15725-D

BOB NICHOLS
See Clayton McMichen

FATE NORRIS
15124-D (as by Fate Norris & The Tanner Boys)
....(Nov 24, 1926)
New Dixie...mx 143047-2
I Don't Reckon That'll Happen Again
....mx 143049-2

15435-D (as by Fate Norris & His Play Boys)
....(Apr 12, 1929)
Roll 'Em On The Ground......................mx 148254-2
Johnnie Get Your Gun..........................mx 148255-2

NORTH CANTON QUARTET
15643-D..(Apr 23, 1930)
I'm Bound For Home............................mx 150366-2
I Want To Live Beyond The Grave............mx 150367-2

NORTH CAROLINA RIDGE RUNNERS
15650-D..(Apr 17, 1928)
Nobody's Darling.................................mx 146106-1
Be Kind To A Man When He's Down.........mx 146107-1

E.B. OWENS
15414-D..(Apr 18, 1929)
Sweet Carlyle......................................mx 148352-1
Goodbye Forever, Darling.....................mx 148353-2

OWENS BROTHERS & ELLIS
15416-D (as by Owens Brothers)
....(Dec 3, 1928)
If You Don't Like My Ford Coupe, Don't You
Cadillac Me...mx 147552-2
Golden Memories Waltz........................mx 147553-2

OWENS BROTHERS & ELLIS

15434-D (as by The Stamps Quartet)
....(Dec 4, 1928)
Delighting In The Love Of God................mx 147556-2
Working For The King Of Kings..............mx 147557-2

15502-D (as by Owens Brothers & Ellis)
....(Dec 4, 1929)
I Worship The Lord............................mx 149522-2
I Want To Do My Best........................mx 149524-2

15560-D (as by Owens Brothers & Ellis)
....(Dec 4, 1929)
You Shall Reap What You Sow...............mx 149528-2
He's Calling All.................................mx 149529-2

15655-D (as by Owens Brothers & Ellis)
....(Dec 4, 1929)
I Am O'ershadowed By Love..................mx 149523-2
He's Calling All.................................mx 149525-2

15242-D (as by The Stamps Quartet)
....(Dec 2, 1927)
In The City Where There Is No Night..........mx 145308-2
I Am Going Over There........................mx 145309-1

15347-D (as by The Stamps Quartet)
....(Dec 3, 1928)
Coming...mx 147550-2
Go On, We'll Soon Be There...................mx 147551-2

PARAMOUNT QUARTET
15020-D...(Jan 30, 1925)
What Did He Do?.................................mx 140309-2
Heaven Is My Home.............................mx 140310-2

CHARLIE PARKER & MACK WOOLBRIGHT
15154-D..(Apr 6, 1927)
Give That Nigger Ham..........................mx 143918-2
Rabbit Chase.....................................mx 143919-2

15236-D...(Nov 10, 1927)
The Man Who Wrote Home Sweet Home Never Was A
Married Man......................................mx 145194-1
Ticklish Reuben..................................mx 145195-1

CHARLIE PARKER & MACK WOOLBRIGHT
15694-D..(Nov 10, 1927)
The Old Arm Chair................................mx 145196-2
Will, The Weaver..................................mx 145197-1

"CHUBBY" PARKER & His OLD TIME BANJO
15296-D...(Aug 23, 1928)
Down On The Farm..............................mx 146878-2
King Kong Kitchie Kitchie Ki-Mi-O...........mx 146879-2

PEGGY PARKER
15725-D..(Oct 30, 1931)
Memphis..mx 151993-?
See Hinky Myers 15725-D

PELICAN WILDCATS
15755-D
Walkin' Georgia Rose..........mx 151956-1 / Oct 27, 1931
See Charles B. Smith 15755-D

OLD HANK PENNY
15766-D..(June 3, 1932)
My Blue Ridge Mountain Bride.................mx 152203-1
When It's Apple Blossom Time Up in The Berkshires
....mx 152204-1

OBED PICKARD OF STATION WSM, NASHVILLE, TN
15141-D..(Mar 31, 1927)
Bury Me Not On The Lone Prairie.............mx 143827-1
Kitty Wells...mx 143828-1

15246-D..(Mar 31, 1927)
Walking In The Parlor............................mx 143829-2
The Old Gray Horse................................mx 143830-1

JACK PICKELL
15052-D..(Sept 29, 1925)
Old Rugged Cross...................................mx W141008-2
That's Why I Love Him So.....................mx W141010-2

15061-D..(Sept 29, 1925)
When They Ring The Golden Bells............mx 141009-2
Memories (Mother's Song).......................mx 141011-1

JACK PICKELL

15083-D..(Apr 21, 1926)
Is It Well Worth Your Soul?...........................mx 142074-1
The Last Mile Of The Way......................mx 142075-2

15117-D..(Apr 21, 1926)
If I Could Hear My Mother Pray Again..........mx 142072
Don't You Love Your Daddy Too?...................mx 142073

15603-D..(Apr 21, 1926)
The Lily Of The Valley..........................mx 142076-2
My Task...mx 142077-1

CHARLIE POOLE With The NORTH CAROLINA RAMBLERS

15038-D (as by Charlie Poole with The North Carolina Ramblers)
....(July 27, 1925)
Can I Sleep In Your Barn Tonight?................mx 140788-2
Don't Let The Deal Go Down...................mx 140789-1

15043-D (as by Charlie Poole with The North Carolina Ramblers)
....(July 27, 1925)
The Girl I Left In Sunny Tennessee............mx 140786-1
I'm The Man That Rode The Mule Round The World..mx 140787-1

15099-D (as by Charlie Poole with The North Carolina Ramblers)
Monkey On A String..........mx 142638-1 / Sept 17, 1926
White House Blues............mx 142658-2 / Sept 20, 1926

15106-D (North Carolina Ramblers Led By Posey Rorer / North Carolina Ramblers)
(Sept 16, 1926)
Flying Clouds..mx 142627-1
Forks Of Sandy...................................mx 142632-1

15116-D (as by Charlie Poole with The North Carolina Ramblers)
Leaving Home..................mx 142645-2 / Sept 18, 1926
There'll Come A Time........mx 142657-3 / Sept 20, 1926

CHARLIE POOLE With The NORTH CAROLINA RAMBLERS

15127-D (as by North Carolina Ramblers Led By Posey Rorer)
....(Sept 18, 1926)
Ragtime Annie.....................................mx 142642-1
Too Young To Marry............................mx 142641-1

15138-D (as by Charlie Poole with The North Carolina Ramblers)
Goodbye Booze.................mx 142637-1 / Sept 17, 1926
Budded Rose....................mx 142646-1 / Sept 18, 1926

15160-D (as by Charlie Poole with The North Carolina Ramblers)
....(Sept 20, 1926)
The Highwayman................................mx 142659-1
Hungry Has House...............................mx 142660-1

15179-D (as by Charlie Poole with The North Carolina Ramblers)
....(July 25, 1927)
The Letter That Never Came..................mx 144514-3
Falling By The Wayside...................mx 144516-1

15184-D (as by Charlie Poole)............(July 26, 1927)
Sunset March......................................mx 144518-1
Don't Let Your Deal Go Down Medley.......mx 144521-2

15193-D (as by Charlie Poole with The North Carolina Ramblers)..(July 25, 1927)
You Ain't Talkin' To Me........................mx 144511-1
Take A Drink On Me............................mx 144515-1

15215-D (as by Charlie Poole with The North Carolina Ramblers)
....(July 25, 1927)
If I Lose, I Don't Care..........................mx 144509-1
Coon From Tennessee...........................mx 145512-2

15279-D (North Carolina Ramblers Led By Posey Rorer / North Carolina Ramblers)
....(Sept 16, 1926)
Wild Horse...mx 142631-1
Mountain Reel....................................mx 142633-2

CHARLIE POOLE With The NORTH CAROLINA RAMBLERS

15286-D (as by Charlie Poole with The North Carolina Ramblers)
....(July 23, 1928)
Ramblin' Blues................................mx 146773-1
Shootin' Creek................................mx 146779-2

15307-D (as by Charlie Poole with The North Carolina Ramblers)
....(July 23, 1928)
I Cannot Call Her Mother....................mx 146769-2
What Is Home Without Babies...............mx 146775-1

15342-D (as by Charlie Poole with The North Carolina Ramblers)
....(July 23, 1928)
Husband And Wife Were Angry One Night
....mx 146771-2
Jealous Mary...................................mx 146776-2

15385-D (as by Charlie Poole with The North Carolina Ramblers)
....(July 23, 1928)
I Onced Loved A Sailor......................mx 146770-2
Hangman, Hangman, Slack The Rope.........mx 146772-1

15407-D (as by Charlie Poole with The North Carolina Ramblers)
Bill Mason......................mx 148469-3 / May 6, 1929
He Rambled....................mx 148476-2 / May 7, 1929

15425-D (as by Charlie Poole with The North Carolina Ramblers)
Leaving Dear Old Ireland......mx 148477-1 / May 6, 1929
Sweet Sunny South..............mx 148475-2 / May 7, 1929

15456-D (as by Charlie Poole with The North Carolina Ramblers)
Good-Bye Mary Dear...........mx 148470-1 / May 6, 1929
The Wayward Boy...............mx 148474-1 / May 7, 1929

15509-D (as by Charlie Poole with The North Carolina Ramblers)
Baltimore Fire....................mx 148472-1 / May 6, 1929
The Mother's Plea For Her Son
....mx 148477-1 / May 7, 1929

CHARLIE POOLE With The NORTH CAROLINA RAMBLERS

15519-D (as by Charlie Poole with The North Carolina Ramblers)
....(Jan 23, 1930)
Sweet Sixteen......................................mx 149900-1
My Gypsy Girl....................................mx 149901-2

15545-D (as by Charlie Poole with The North Carolina Ramblers)
....(Jan 23, 1930)
If The River Was Whiskey.....................mx 149906-1
It's Movin' Day..................................mx 149907-1

15584-D (as by Charlie Poole with The North Carolina Ramblers)
....(July 23, 1928)
A Young Boy Left His Home One Day.......mx 146767-2
My Wife Went Away And Left Me............mx 46768-2

15601-D (as by Charlie Poole with The North Carolina Ramblers)
....(Sept 9, 1930)
Goodbye Sweet Liza Jane......................mx 150773-1
Look Before You Leap..........................mx 150774-2

15615-D (as by Charlie Poole & Roy Harvey)
....(Jan 23, 1930)
Southern Medley.................................mx 149908-1
Honeysuckle.......................................mx 149909-3

15636-D (as by Charlie Poole with The North Carolina Ramblers)
....(Sept 9, 1930)
Just Keep Waiting Till The Good Times Come
....mx 150777-2
Wher The Whippoorwill Is Whispering Goodnight
....mx 150780-2

15672-D (as by Charlie Poole with The North Carolina Ramblers)
....(July 23, 1928)
Took My Gal A Walkin'.........................mx 146774-2
Old And Only in The Way......................mx 146778-1

CHARLIE POOLE With The NORTH CAROLINA RAMBLERS

15688-D (as by Charlie Poole with The North Carolina Ramblers)
....(Sept 9, 1930)
One Moonlight Night............................mx 150775-2
Milwaukee Blues..................................mx 150779-2

15711-D (as by Charlie Poole with The North Carolina Ramblers)
....(Jan 23, 1930)
The Only Girl I Ever Loved....................mx 149902-1
Write A Letter To My Mother.................mx 149904-2

PRAETORIAN QUARTET

15384-D...(Dec 9, 1928)
Is It Well With Your Soul.......................mx 147618-1
At Sunset I'm Going Home....................mx 147619-2

PROXIMITY STRING QUARTET

15533-D...(Oct 16, 1928)
Lindy...mx 147196-2
Louise...mx 147197-1

REUBEN PUCKETT (Richard Brooks)

15029-D...(Jan 29, 1925)
Always Think Of Mother.......................mx 140296-1
Down By The Mississippi Shore..............mx 140297-1

RILEY PUCKETT

15003-D (as by Riley Puckett)
....(Sept 12, 1924)
Spanish Cavalier.................................mx 140030-1
Swanee River.....................................mx 140027-2

15004-D (as by Riley Puckett)
....(Sept 11, 1924)
We'll Sow Righteous Seed For The Reaper
....mx 140010-1
Where Is My Wandering Boy Tonight
....mx 140011-2

15005-D (as by Riley Puckett)
....(Sept 11, 1924)
Old Black Joe.....................................mx 140014-2
When You And I Were Young, Maggie......mx 140026-2

RILEY PUCKETT

15014-D (as by Riley Puckett)
....(Sept 11, 1924)
Old Susanna...mx 140024-2
Liza Jane..mx 130018-1

15015-D (as by Riley Puckett)
....(Sept 12, 1924)
Burglar Man...mx 140029-2
When I Had But Fifty Cents.................mx 140028-1

15033-D (as by Riley Puckett)
Old Joe Clark....................mx 81603-3 / Mar 7, 1924
Jesse James..................mx 140016 -1 / Sept 11, 1924

15035-D (as by Riley Puckett)
....(June 15, 1925)
Drunkards Dream...............................mx W140669 -2
Just Break The News To Mother............mx W140668-2

15036-D (as by Riley Puckett)
I Wish I Was Single Again
...................................mx W140670-3 / June 15, 1925
It's Simple To Flirt
...................................mx W140690-2 / June 16, 1925

15040-D (as by Riley Puckett)
....(Sept 11, 1924)
Whoa Mule..mx 140021-2
Railroad Bill..mx 140023-2

15045-D (as by Riley Puckett)
....(Sept 30, 1925)
The Preacher And The Bear..................mx W141061-3
Long Tongue Woman..........................mx W141062 -1

15050-D (as by Riley Puckett)
....(Oct 2, 1925)
Boston Burglar....................................mx W141081-2
Orphan Girl..mx W141082-1

15055-D (as by Riley Puckett)
....(Sept 30, 1925)
When I'm Gone, You'll Soon Forget........mx W141067-1
When I'm Gone You Won't Forget.........mx W141066-1

RILEY PUCKETT

15058-D (as by Riley Puckett)
....(Sept 30, 1925)
Down By The Old Mill Stream...............mx W141065-2
Won't You Come Over To My House......mx W141064-2

15063-D (as by Riley Puckett)
...............................…......................(Oct 2, 1925)
I'll Never Get Drunk No More.................mx 141086-2
You'd Be Surprised.............................mx 141085-1

15068-D (as by Riley Puckett)
To Wed You In The Golden Summer Time
.................................mx141063--1 / Sept 30, 1925
Hello Central, Give Me Heaven
......................................mx 141083-2 / Oct 2, 1925

15073-D (as by Riley Puckett)
Send Back My Wedding Ring
......................................mx 141080-1 / Oct 2, 1925
Wait Till The Sun Shines, Nellie
....................................mx 140647-1 / June 16, 1925

15078-D (as by Riley Puckett)
....(Apr 20, 1926)
Wal I Swan...............................mx142054 -1
Everybody Works But Father.............mx142057-1

15088-D (as by Riley Puckett)
....(Apr 20, 1926)
Rock-A-Bye Baby...............................mx 142055-2
Sauerkraut..mx 142056-1

15102-D (as by Riley Puckett)
....(Apr 22, 1926)
Sally Goodwin............................mx 142086-2
Ida Red......................................mx 142087-1

15125-D (as by Riley Puckett)
Put My Little Shoes Away
.................................mx 142059-2 / Apr 20, 1926
Take Me Back To My Carolina Home
....................................mx 143103-2 / Nov 6, 1926

15139-D (as by Riley Puckett)
Jack And Jill...................mx 142058-2 / Apr 20, 1926
Down In Arkansas.............mx 142088-1 / Apr 22, 1926

RILEY PUCKETT

15163-D (as by Riley Puckett)
....(Apr 2, 1927)
Fuzzy Rag..mx 143871-2
The Darkey's Wail...............................mx 143872-1

15171-D (as by Riley Puckett)
....(Apr 1, 1927)
Little Log Cabin In The Lane...................mx 143858-1
Sleep Baby Sleep..................................mx 143857-2

15185-D (as by Riley Puckett)
....(Apr 1, 1927)
Alabama Gal...mx 143856-2
Fire On The Mountain...........................mx 143855-2

15196-D (as by Riley Puckett)
....(Nov 6, 1926)
My Puppy Bud....................................mx 143105-2
My Poodle Dog...................................mx 143102--2

15226-D (as by Riley Puckett)
....(Oct 31, 1927)
Come Be My Rainbow....................mx 145045--2
Red Wing...................................mx 145043-2

15250-D (as by Riley Puckett)
....(Nov 4, 1927)
All Bound Round With The Mason Dixon Line
....mx 145110-2
Mother..mx 145111-1

15261-D (as by Riley Puckett)
....(Apr 11, 1928)
Mama Won't Allow No Low Down Hanging Around
....mx 146012-1
Blue Yodel No. 1.................................mx 146013-2

15277-D (as by Riley Puckett)
....(Apr 14, 1928)
Little Maumee....................................mx 146068-2
Breeze..mx 146069-2

RILEY PUCKETT

15324-D (as by Riley Puckett)
Away Out On The Mountain
..............................mx 147258-2 / Oct 22, 1928
The Moonshiner's Dream
..............................mx 147269-2 / Oct 23, 1928

15337-D (as by Hugh Cross & Riley Puckett)
Call Me Back Pal O' Mine
..............................mx 147244-2 / Oct 22, 1928
Clover Blossoms.........mx 147265-2 / Oct 23, 1928

15374-D (as by Riley Puckett)
....(Oct 23, 1928)
I'm Going To Georgia...........................mx 147273-1
On The Other Side Of Jordan...................mx 147268-2

15392-D (as by Riley Puckett)
I'm Going Where The Chilly Winds Don't Blow
..............................mx 145044-2 / Oct 31, 1927
Don't Try It For It Can't Be Done
..............................mx 147257-2 / Oct 22, 1928

15393-D (as by Riley Puckett)
....(Apr 10, 1929)
Carolina Moon.................................mx 148234-2
Will You Ever Think Of me....................mx 148235-2

15408-D (as by Riley Puckett)
Waiting For a Train............mx 148233-2 / Apr 10, 1929
I'm Up In The Air About Mary
..............................mx 148244-2 / Apr 11, 1929

15448-D (as by Riley Puckett)
....(Apr 11, 1929)
Don't Let Your Deal Go Down................mx 148242-2
McKinley..mx 148243-1

15505-D (as by Riley Puckett)
Dissatisfied.....................mx 149295-1 / Oct 30, 1929
Frankie And Johnnie (You'll Miss Me In The Days To Come)............................mx 149364-1 / Nov 4, 1929

15563-D (as by Riley Puckett)
....(Apr 16, 1930)
Nine Hundred Miles From Home..............mx 150243-2
Dark Town Strutter's Ball......................mx 150246-2

RILEY PUCKETT

15605-D (as by Riley Puckett)
....Apr 14, 1930)
Waitin' For The Evening Mail..................mx 150208-2
Ramblin' Boy...mx 150209-2

15631-D (as by Riley Puckett)
Moonlight On The Colorado
....mx 151049-1 / Dec 5, 1930
Somewhere In Old Wyoming
....mx 151094-1 / Dec 8, 1930

15656-D (as by Riley Puckett)
The Cat Came Back.............mx 151050-2 / Dec 5, 1930
Beaver Cap.......................mx 151095-1 / Dec 8, 1930

15686-D (as by Riley Puckett & Clayton McMichen)
....(Oct 26, 1928)
Farmer's Daughter..............................mx 147298-2
The Arkansas Sheik............................mx 147300-2

15708-D (as by Riley Puckett)
....(Apr 16, 1930)
There's A Hard Time Coming..................mx 150244-2
Paw's Old Mule..................................mx 150245-2

15719-D (as by Riley Puckett)
....(Oct 29, 1931)
Twenty One Years..............................mx 151980-1
All Bound Down In Prison......................mx 151981-1

15747-D (as by Riley Puckett)
....(Oct 29, 1931)
East Bound Train................................mx 151978-1
Careless Love...................................mx 151979-1

15774-D (as by Bill Helms & Riley Puckett / Colon Jones & Riley Puckett)
Lost Love.......................mx 149288-2 / Oct 29, 1929
That Saxophone Waltz.........mx 149303-2 / Oct 30, 1929

RAINEY OLD TIME BAND

15675-D...(Dec 15, 1928)
Engineer Frank Hawk...........................mx 147648-2
Crawford March.................................mx 147649-1

GROVER RANN & HARRY AYERS

15600-D...(Apr 23, 1930)
They Tell Me Love's A Pleasure...............mx 150372-2
Little Dolly Driftwood...........................mx 150373-2

15638-D...(Dec 6, 1930)
Don't Stay After Ten............................mx 151070-2
I'se Gwine Back To Dixie......................mx 151072-1

RECTOR TRIO

15658-D...(Dec 3, 1930)
Skyland Rag.......................................mx 151006-2
Mount Pisgah Blues.............................mx 151007-1

RED MOUNTAIN TRIO (Jimmy Yates)

15260-D...(Apr 20, 1928)
The Wang Wang Blues.........................mx 146163-2
Home Again Medley............................mx 146164-1

15369-D...(Oct 31, 1928)
Salting Down The Chesapeake Bay...........mx 147362-1
Dixie...mx 147363-2

15462-D...(Oct 31, 1928)
Carolina Sunshine................................mx 147364-1
Gypsy Love Song (Slumber On, My Little Gypsy
Sweetheart)..mx 147365-2

BILL & BELLE REED

15336-D...(Oct 17, 1928)
You Shall Be Free................................mx 147210-2
Old Lady And The Devil.......................mx 147211-2

THE REED CHILDREN

15525-D...(Oct 17, 1928)
I'll Be All Smiles Tonight......................mx 147212-2
I Once Did Have A Sweetheart...............mx 147213-2

REMUS RICH & CARL BRADSHAW

15341-D...(Oct 15, 1928)
Goodbye Sweetheart............................mx 147186-2
Sleep Baby Sleep.................................mx 147187-1

FRED RICHARDS

15483-D...(Oct 23, 1929)
My Katie..mx 149246-2
Danville Blues....................................mx 149247-2

ROANE COUNTY RAMBLERS
15328-D..(Oct 15, 1928)
Home Town Blues................................mx 147182-2
Southern No. 111.................................mx 147183-2

15377-D..(Oct 15, 1928)
Step High Waltz..................................mx 147184-1
Tennessee Waltz..................................mx 147185-1

15398-D..(Apr 15, 1929)
Roane County Rag...............................mx 148283-2
Everybody Two Step............................mx 148284-1

15438-D..(Apr 15, 1929)
McCaroll's Breakdown..........................mx 148279-2
Green River March...............................mx 148280-2

15498-D..(Oct 21, 1929)
Free A Little Bird.................................mx 149208-1
Johnson City Rag.................................mx 149209-2

15570-D..(Oct 21, 1929)
Callahan Rag.......................................mx 149210-2
Alabama Trot......................................mx 149211-2

GEORGE ROARK
15383-D..(Oct 18, 1928)
I Ain't A Bit Drunk..............................mx 147230-1
My Old Coon Dog................................mx 147231-1

CARSON ROBISON / FRANK LUTHER
15532-D (as by George Thompson (pseudonym for Frank Luther)
....(Feb 26, 1930)
Cross Eyed Sue....................................mx 150021-2
A Chaw Of Tabacco And A Little Drink.......mx 150022-3

15547-D (as by Travelin' Jim Smith)......(Apr 14, 1930)
So I Joined The Navy............................mx 150461-2
Naw! I Don't Wanta Be Rich...................mx 150462-2

15548-D (as by Carson Robison)
....(Apr 25, 1930)
Ohio Prison Fire...................................mx 150491-2
Why Are The Young Folks So Thoughtless
....mx 150492-3

CARSON ROBISON / FRANK LUTHER

15588-D (as by Frank Luther & Carson Robison)
....(Aug 4, 1930)
Carry Me Back To The Mountains............mx 150686-1
Oklahoma Charley...............................mx 150687-1

15627-D (as by Carson Robison & Phil Crow / Carson Robison & Frank Luther)
....(Dec 3, 1930)
Abraham......................................mx150951-3
I'm Gittin' ready To Go................mx 150999-2

15644-D (as by Carson Robison & Frank Luther)
....(Dec3, 1930)
My Heart Is Where The Mohawk Flows Tonight
....mx 150995-2
Sleepy Hollow...............................mx 150996-2

15768-D (as by Black Brothers / Carson Robison & Frank Luther)
....(Oct 20, 1930)
Carry Me Back To The Mountains............mx 404493-B
I'll Never See My Darling Anymore..........mx 404494-B

15773-D (as by Carson Robison & His Pioneers)
....(Apr 1932)
Old Familiar Tunes Part 1 .... mx 130891-1
Old Familiar Tunes Part 2.......................mx 130892-1

15779-D (as by Carson Robison & Frank Luther)
Missouri Valley.................mx 151822-2 / Sept 30, 1931
When It's Springtime In The Blue Ridge Mountains
...................................mx 152102-1 / Feb 3, 1932

ROE BROTHER'S & MORRELL

15156-D..(Mar 28, 1927)
The Ship That Never Returned..................mx 143781-1
She'll Be Coming Around The Mountain
....mx 143783-1

15199-D..(Mar 28, 1927)
Goin' Down The Road Feeling Bad...........mx 143779-1
My Little Mohi....................................mx 143782-2

ERNEST ROGERS
15012-D..(Jan 30, 1925)
My Red Haired Lady............................mx 140305-2
Willie The Weeper...............................mx 140304-2

ROPER'S MOUNTAIN SINGERS
15222-D..(Nov 2, 1927)
When I Walked The Streets Of Gold...........mx 145078-2
On The Sea Of Life...............................mx 145079-1

ROYAL SUMNER QUARTET
15233-D..(Apr 2, 1927)
Fight To Win.......................................mx 143877-2
Be A Man..mx 143878-1

SAWYER SISTERS (Celia & Ann)
15745-D..(Oct 26, 1931)
It's All In The Game............................mx 151947-1
See Duncan Sisters 15745-D

SHAMROCK STRING BAND
15339-D..(Oct 22, 1928)
Kuhala March.....................................mx 147245-1
High Low March..................................mx 147246-2

15534-D..(Oct 22, 1928)
Hawaiian Moon Waltz...........................mx 147247-1
Sweetheart Waltz.................................mx 147248-1

THE SHELBY SINGERS
See Bob Miller 15760-D

SHELL CREEK QUARTET
15355-D..(Oct 15, 1928)
My Boyhood Days................................mx 147176-1
Back Where The Old Home Stands............mx 147177-1

EARL SHIRKEY & ROY HARPER (pseudonym for Roy Harvey)
15326-D (as by Earl Shirkey & Roy Harper)
....(Oct 18, 1928)
Steamboat Man...................................mx 147226-2
When The Roses Bloom For The Bootlegger
....mx 147227-1

EARL SHIRKEY & ROY HARPER (pseudonym for Roy Harvey)

15376-D (as by Earl Shirkey & Roy Harper)
....(Oct 18, 1928)
Poor Little Joe......................................mx 147228-1
We Parted At The Gate.........................mx 147229-2

15406-D (as by Roy Harper & Earl Shirkey)
....(Mar 26, 1929)
The Yodeling Mule...............................mx 148130-2
The Railroad Blues...............................mx 148136-1

15429-D (as by Roy Harper & Earl Shirkey)
....(Mar 26, 1929)
The Bootlegger's Dream Of Home.............mx 148135-2
Keep Bachelor's Hall............................mx 148137-2

15467-D (as by Roy Harper & Earl Shirkey)
....(Mar 26, 1929)
The Cowboy's Lullaby..........................mx 148134-1
Kitty Waltz Yodel................................mx 148138-2

15490-D (as by Earl Shirkey & Roy Harper)
....(Oct 22, 1929)
My Yodeling Sweetheart........................mx 149228-2
I'm Longing To Belong To Someone..........mx 149229-1

15535-D (as by Earl Shirkey & Roy Harper)
....(Oct 22, 1929)
The Virginian Strike Of '23....................mx 149226-1
A Hobo's Pal.......................................mx 149231-2

15642-D (as by Earl Shirkey & Roy Harper)
....(Oct 22, 1929)
The Policeman's Little Child...................mx 149227-2
We Have Moonshine In The West Virginia Hills
....mx 149230-2

BILL SHORES & MELVIN DUPREE

15506-D..(Oct 30, 1929)
Wedding Bells....................................mx 149306-2
West Texas Breakdown..........................mx 149307-1

ERNEST ROGERS
15012-D..(Jan 30, 1925)
My Red Haired Lady.............................mx 140305-2
Willie The Weeper................................mx 140304-2

ROPER'S MOUNTAIN SINGERS
15222-D..(Nov 2, 1927)
When I Walked The Streets Of Gold...........mx 145078-2
On The Sea Of Life................................mx 145079-1

ROYAL SUMNER QUARTET
15233-D..(Apr 2, 1927)
Fight To Win.......................................mx 143877-2
Be A Man..mx 143878-1

SAWYER SISTERS (Celia & Ann)
15745-D..(Oct 26, 1931)
It's All In The Game.............................mx 151947-1
See Duncan Sisters 15745-D

SHAMROCK STRING BAND
15339-D..(Oct 22, 1928)
Kuhala March......................................mx 147245-1
High Low March..................................mx 147246-2

15534-D..(Oct 22, 1928)
Hawaiian Moon Waltz...........................mx 147247-1
Sweetheart Waltz..................................mx 147248-1

THE SHELBY SINGERS
See Bob Miller 15760-D

SHELL CREEK QUARTET
15355-D..(Oct 15, 1928)
My Boyhood Days.................................mx 147176-1
Back Where The Old Home Stands............mx 147177-1

EARL SHIRKEY & ROY HARPER (pseudonym for Roy Harvey)
15326-D **(as by Earl Shirkey & Roy Harper)**
....(Oct 18, 1928)
Steamboat Man....................................mx 147226-2
When The Roses Bloom For The Bootlegger
....mx 147227-1

EARL SHIRKEY & ROY HARPER (pseudonym for Roy Harvey)

15376-D (as by Earl Shirkey & Roy Harper)
....(Oct 18, 1928)
Poor Little Joe....................................mx 147228-1
We Parted At The Gate.......................mx 147229-2

15406-D (as by Roy Harper & Earl Shirkey)
....(Mar 26, 1929)
The Yodeling Mule.............................mx 148130-2
The Railroad Blues.............................mx 148136-1

15429-D (as by Roy Harper & Earl Shirkey)
....(Mar 26, 1929)
The Bootlegger's Dream Of Home.............mx 148135-2
Keep Bachelor's Hall..........................mx 148137-2

15467-D (as by Roy Harper & Earl Shirkey)
....(Mar 26, 1929)
The Cowboy's Lullaby........................mx 148134-1
Kitty Waltz Yodel..............................mx 148138-2

15490-D (as by Earl Shirkey & Roy Harper)
....(Oct 22, 1929)
My Yodeling Sweetheart......................mx 149228-2
I'm Longing To Belong To Someone.........mx 149229-1

15535-D (as by Earl Shirkey & Roy Harper)
....(Oct 22, 1929)
The Virginian Strike Of '23...................mx 149226-1
A Hobo's Pal.....................................mx 149231-2

15642-D (as by Earl Shirkey & Roy Harper)
....(Oct 22, 1929)
The Policeman's Little Child..................mx 149227-2
We Have Moonshine In The West Virginia Hills
....mx 149230-2

BILL SHORES & MELVIN DUPREE

15506-D..(Oct 30, 1929)
Wedding Bells...................................mx 149306-2
West Texas Breakdown.......................mx 149307-1

CONNIE SIDES
15008-D
You're As Welcome As The Flowers In May
.................................mx 81995--1 / Sept 10, 1924
They Made It Twice As Nice
.................................mx 81999-1 / Sept 11, 1924

15009-D.......................................(Sept 10, 1924)
Underneath The Sugar Moon....................mx 81994-2
In The Shadow Of The Pines....................mx 81996-1
See Ernest Thompson 15002-D

OLIVER SIMS
15103-D.......................................(Apr 24, 1926)
Lost John..mx 142129-2
Hop About Ladies...............................mx 142128-1

BUD SKIDMORE
See Bob Miller 15761-D

CHARLES B. SMITH
15755-D
My Little A-1 Brownie.........mx 151654-1 / June 26, 1931
See Pelican Wildcats 15755-D

J. FRANK SMITH
See Smith's Sacred Singers 15137-D

MARSHALL SMITH & JOHN MARLOR
15080-D.......................................(Apr 21, 1926)
Jonah And The Whale..........................mx 142070-2
Home In The Rock..............................mx 142071-2

MERRITT SMITH & LEO BOSWELL
15748-D.......................................(Oct 28, 1931)
My Hearts Turned Back to Dixie...............mx 151972-1
Try Not To Forget...............................mx 151974-1

SMITH'S SACRED SINGERS
15090-D.......................................(Apr 23, 1926)
Picture From Life's Other Side................mx 142094-1
Where We'll Never Grow Old..................mx 142095-2

15110-D.......................................(Nov 3, 1926)
The Eastern Gate................................mx 14033-1
Shouting On The Hill...........................mx 143036-1

SMITH'S SACRED SINGERS

15128-D
We're Going Down The Valley One By One
................................mx 143016-3 / Nov 2, 1926
If I'm Faithful To My Lord
................................mx 143037-1 / Nov 3, 1926

15137-D **(as by J. Frank Smith)**..............(Nov 3, 1926)
The Prodigals Return...........................mx 143035-2
The Drunkard's Child...........................mx 143039-1

15144-D...(Apr 4, 1927)
I Will Sing Of My Redeemer....................mx 143885-2
He Will Set Your Fields On Fire...............mx 143886-2

15159-D
Jesus Prayed......................mx 143034-2 / Nov 3, 1926
Life's Railway To Heaven......mx 143908-1 / Apr 5, 1927

15173-D...(Apr 4, 1927)
Trace The Footsteps Of Jesus..................mx 143887-2
He is Coming Back..............................mx 143889-2

15195-D...(Apr 5, 1927)
City Of Gold.....................................mx 143906-2
Climbing Up The Golden Stairs................mx 143910-1

15208-D...(Nov 7, 1927)
Gospel Waves...................................mx 145145-2
He Bore It All...................................mx 145146-2

15230-D...(Nov 7, 1927)
We Shall Rise...................................mx 145149-2
I Want To Go To Heaven.......................mx145148-2

15257-D...(Apr 17, 1928)
Let The Lower Lights Be Burning.............mx 146110-2
Drifting Down..................................mx 146113-2

15281-D...(Apr 17, 1928)
Prepare To Meet My God......................mx 146114-1
My Latest Sun Is Sinking Fast.................mx 146115-2

15308-D...(Apr 17, 1928)
Waiting On The Golden Shore................mx 146112-2
Hold To God's Unchanging Hand..............mx 14611-2

SMITH'S SACRED SINGERS

15329-D..(Oct 30, 1928)
Deliverance Will Come..........................mx 147350-1
The Home Over There...........................mx 147352-1

15351-D
Keep On Climbing...............mx 145144-2 / Nov 7, 1927
The Unclouded Day............mx 147348-1 / Oct 30, 1928

15371-D..(Oct 30, 1928)
Lord I'm Coming Home........................mx 147353-2
When Jesus Comes...............................mx 147351-2

15389-D
I Am Going That Way..........mx 145150-2 / Nov 7, 1927
When The Happy Morning Breaks
....mx 147349-1 / Oct 30, 1928

15401-D..(Apr 17, 1929)
Working For The Crown........................mx 148341-2
Meet Me There....................................mx 148345-2

15430-D..(Apr 17, 1929)
Are You Washed In The Blood Of The Lamb
....mx 148338-2
Jesus Died For Me................................mx 148339-2

15471-D..(Apr 17, 1929)
Endless Joy Is Waiting Over There............mx 148340-2
What A Gathering That Will Be................mx 148346-2

15494-D..(Nov 5, 1929)
When Our Saviour Comes Again...............mx 149385-2
His Picture Is In My Heart.......................mx 149386-1

15517-D..(Nov 5, 1929)
You Can't Do Wrong And Get By.............mx 149379-2
Labor On...mx 149380-2

15551-D..(Apr 18, 1930)
The Church In The Wildwood..................mx 150285-2
There Is A Fountain Filled With Blood.........mx150289-1

15579-D..(Nov 5, 1929)
He Holds Me By The Hand.....................mx 149381-2
Echoes From The Glory Shore..................mx 149384-2

SMITH'S SACRED SINGERS

15593-D..(Apr 18, 1930)
Jesus Lover Of My Soul.........................mx 150287-1
Work For The Night Is Coming...............mx 150288-1

15619-D..(Apr 18, 1930)
Love Lifted Me......................................mx 150283-2
How Firm A Foundation........................mx 150290-2

15626-D..(Oct 25, 1928)
Life's Troubled Sea...............................mx 147291-2
Just Over In The Glory Land..................mx 147292-1

15639-D..(Dec 4, 1930)
Old Time Religion For Me.....................mx 151033-1
My Redeemer Lives...............................mx 151034-2

15659-D..(Dec 4, 1930)
Sing All Your Troubles Away.................mx 151029-1
Wayside Wells.......................................mx 151031-2

15671-D..(Apr 5, 1927)
A Child At Mother's Knee......................mx 143904-2
Beautiful Life...mx 143905-2

15683-D..(Dec 4, 1930)
In A Little While....................................mx 151030-1
It Won't Be Long...................................mx 151032-1

15706-D..(Apr 18, 1930)
Is It Well With Your Soul......................mx 150284-2
Gathering Home....................................mx 150286-2

15749-D..(Nov 5, 1929)
My Saviour's Train................................mx 149382-1
I Have Found The Way..........................mx 149383-2

15772-D..(Apr 17, 1929)
Keep The Sunlight In Your Sky..............mx 148344-?
When Our Lord Shall Come Again.........mx 148347-?

SNOWBALL & SUNSHINE

15722-D..(Nov 3, 1931)
Leave it There.......................................mx 152021-1
When The Saints Go Marching In..........mx 152022-1

SNOWBALL & SUNSHINE

15738-D **(as by Rev. Snowball)**..............(Nov 3, 1931)
Moses And The Bull Rush Part 1...............mx 152029-1
Moses And The Bull Rush Part 2...............mx 152030-1

THE SPINDALE QUARTET

15488-D...(Oct 22, 1929)
Face To Face..mx 149222-2
Lift Him Up...mx 149223-2

15541-D...(Oct 22, 1929)
Sweet Peace The Gift Of God's Love.........mx 149220-2
God Will Take Care Of You....................mx 149221-1

THE SPOONEY FIVE

15234-D...(Nov 8, 1927)
Chinese Rag..mx 145172-1
My Little Girl......................................mx 145173-2

FRED STANLEY

15559-D...(Apr 15, 1930)
The Tie That Binds...............................mx 150224-1
The Cottage By The Sea.........................mx 150225-2

STAPLETON BROTHERS

15284-D...(Apr 19, 1928)
Call Of The Whip-Poor-Will....................mx 146140-1
In A Cool Shady Nook...........................mx 146141-1

UNCLE BUNT STEPHENS

15071-D...(Mar 29, 1926)
Louisburg Blues...................................mx 141874-1
Sail Away Lady...................................mx 141876-2

15085-D...(Mar 29, 1926)
Candy Girl...mx 141877-3
Left In The Dark Blues..........................mx 141875-3

CHARLES LEWIS STINE

15027-D...(Mar 19, 1925)
Ship That Never Returned......................mx 140448-1
Wreck Of The C & O.............................mx 140447-1

LOWE STOKES

15241-D (as by Lowe Stokes & His North Georgians)
....(Oct 31, 1927)
Home Brew Rag.................................mx 145051-3
Unexplained Blues.............................mx 145052-2

15367-D (as by Lowe Stokes & His North Georgians)
....(Oct 27, 1928)
Wave That Frame..............................mx 147312-2
Take Me To The Land Of Jazz................mx 147313-2

15486-D (as by Lowe Stokes & Mike Whitten)
....(Oct 30, 1929)
Katy Did...mx 149297-2
Take Me Back to Georgia.....................mx 149298-2

15557-D (as by Lowe Stokes & His North Georgians)
....(Nov 1, 1929)
Left All Alone Again Blues....................mx 149332-2
Wish I Had Stayed In The Wagon Yard
....mx 149333-1

15606-D (as by Lowe Stokes & His North Georgians)
....(Nov 1, 1929)
Sailin' Down The Chesapeake Bay ....mx 149330-2
Everybody's Doing It..........................mx 149331-2

15620-D (as by Lowe Stokes & Riley Puckett)
....(Apr 14, 1930)
Sally Johnson...................................mx 150206-2
Billy In The Low Ground.....................mx 150207-2

15660-D (as by Lowe Stokes & His North Georgians)
....(Apr 22, 1930)
Bone Dry Blues.................................mx 150350-2
It Just Suits Me.................................mx 150351-2

15693-D (as by Lowe Stokes & His North Georgians)
....(Dec 7, 1930)
Row, Row, Row................................mx 151079-2
Sailing On The Robert E. Lee.................mx 151080-1

STOVEPIPE #1 (pseudonym for Sam Jones)
15011-D..(Oct 1924)
Fisher's Hornpipe...............................mx 81941-?
Lonesome John.................................mx 81937-?

STRINGFELLOW QUARTET
15726-D..(Oct 26, 1931)
We'll Reap What we Sow........................mx 151939-1
I Want to Hear Him Call My Name............mx 141940-1

STROUP QUARTET
15299-D..(Apr 20, 1928)
The Man Behind The Plow.....................mx 146155-2
Dreaming...mx 146156-2

SUNSHINE FOUR
15119-D..(Nov 4, 1926)
In My Heart..mx 143070-1
Beautiful Land....................................mx 143071-1

BERT SWOR & DICK MACK
15707-D..(Sept 15, 1931)
Wowdy Dowdy Part 1............................mx 151788-1
Wowdy Dowdy Part 2............................mx 151789-1

15718-D..(Sept 28, 1931)
Wowdy Dowdy Part 3............................mx 151814-1
Wowdy Dowdy Part 4............................mx 151815-1

15743-D..(Sept 28, 1931)
Wowdy Dowdy Part 5............................mx 151816-1
Wowdy Dowdy Part 6............................mx 151817-1

ARTHUR TANNER & His CORNSHUCKERS
15145-D (as by Arthur Tanner & His Cornshuckers
....(Apr 1, 1927)
Jealous Lover.....................................mx 143851-2
Knoxville Girl......................................mx 143852-2

15180-D (as by Arthur Tanner & His Cornshuckers / Arthur Tanner)
....(Apr 1, 1927)
Shack No. 9..mx 143850-2
Two Little Children...............................mx 143853-1

15352-D (as by Arthur Tanner & His Cornshuckers)
....(Apr 17, 1928)
The Disappointed Lover........................mx 146108-2
Sleep On Blue Eyes.............................mx 146109-2

ARTHUR TANNER & His CORNSHUCKERS

15479-D (as by Arthur Tanner & His Cornshuckers)
....(Apr 12, 1929)
Dr. Gunger Blue..................................mx 148268-1
Lay Me Where Sweet Flowers Blossom.......mx 148269-2

15577-D (as by Arthur Tanner & Riley Puckett)
....(Apr 12, 1928)
Bring Back My Blue Eyed Boy.................mx 148264-1
Gather The Flowers............................mx 148265-1

GID TANNER (& His SKILLET-LICKERS)

15010-D (as by Gid Tanner)................(Sept 12, 1924)
Don't Grieve Your Mother......................mx 140051-1
Be Kind To A Man When He's Down.........mx 140048-2

15016-D (as by Gid Tanner)..................(Mar 7, 1924)
Boll Weevil Blues...............................mx 81604--6
I'm Satisfied..mx 81627-1

15017-D (as by Gid Tanner / Gid Tanner & Riley Puckett)
....(Sept 12, 1924)
Fox Chase..mx 140050-1
Arkansas Traveler................................mx 140045-1

15019-D (as by Gid Tanner / Gid Tanner & Riley Puckett)
Georgia Railroad...............mx 140019-1 / Sept 11, 1924
John Henry......................mx140031-1 / Sept 12, 1924

15059-D (as by Gid Tanner's Georgia Boys)
....(Oct 3, 1925)
Old Time Tunes................................mx 41087-2
Just Gimme The Leavings.....................mx141088-1

15074-D (as by Gid Tanner & His Skillet Lickers with Riley Puckett)
....(Apr 17, 1926)
Bully Of The Town..............................mx 142035-1
Pass Around The Bottle.........................mx 142036-1

15084-D (as by Gid Tanner & His Skillet Lickers with Riley Puckett)
....(Apr 17, 1926)
Turkey In The Straw............................mx 142041-3
You Gotta Quit Knockin' My Dog Aroun'
....mx 142040-1

GID TANNER (& His SKILLET-LICKERS)

15091D (as by Gid Tanner & His Skillet Lickers with Riley Puckett)
....(Apr 17, 1926)
Hand Me Down My Walking Cane............mx 142034-2
Watermelon On The Vine........................mx 142038-1

15097-D (as by Gid Tanner & Faith Norris)
....(Apr 20, 1926)
S-A-V-E-D..mx 142060-1
Where Did You Get That?............................mx 142061-2

15104-D (as by Gid Tanner & His Skillet Lickers with Riley Puckett)
....(Apr 17, 1926)
Don't You Hear Jerusalem Moan................mx 142039-1
Alabama Jubilee..................................mx 142037-2

15105-D (as by Gid Tanner & Faith Norris)
Goodbye Booze..................mx 142063-1 / Apr 20, 1926
See Dock Walsh 15105-D

15108-D (as by Gid Tanner & His Skillet Lickers with Riley Puckett & Clayton McMichen)
....(Nov 3, 1926)
Dance All Night With A Bottle In Your Hand
....mx 143026-1
Old Joe Clark..mx 143032-1

15123-D (as by Gid Tanner & His Skillet Lickers with Riley Puckett & Clayton McMichen)
....(Nov 3, 1926)
I Don't Love Nobody............................mx 143028-1
Shortening Bread..................................mx 143031-2

15134-D (as by Gid Tanner & His Skillet Lickers with Riley Puckett & Clayton McMichen)
Uncle Bud........................mx 143021-2 / Nov 2, 1926
I Got Mine........................mx 143030-1 / Nov 3, 1926

15142-D (as by Gid Tanner & His Skillet Lickers with Riley Puckett & Clayton McMichen)
Wreck Of The Old 97 Southern
..................................mx 143786-1 / Mar 28, 1927
John Henry, The Steel Drivin' Man
..................................mx 143799-2 / Mar 29, 1927

GID TANNER (& His SKILLET-LICKERS)

15158-D (as by Gid Tanner & His Skillet Lickers with Riley Puckett & Clayton McMichen)
....(Mar 29, 1927)
Dixie..mx 143795-2
Run Nigger Run..........................mx 143796-1

15165-D (as by Gid Tanner & Fate Norris)
....(Mar 31, 1927)
Baby Lou...mx 143826-1
Football Rag....................................mx 143825-2

15170-D (as by Gid Tanner & His Skillet Lickers with Riley Puckett & Clayton McMichen)
....(Mar 29, 1927)
Old Gray Mare................................mx 143798-2
The Girl I Left Behind Me......................mx 143797-2

15188-D (as by Gid Tanner & His Skillet Lickers with Riley Puckett & Clayton McMichen)
....(Mar 29, 1927)
Drink Er Down................................mx 143800-2
Darktown Strutter's Ball........................mx 143801-2

15200-D (as by Gid Tanner's Skillet Lickers)
Polly Woddle Doo..............mx 143019-1 / Nov 2, 1926
She'll Be Coming Round The Mountain
...................................mx 143027-1 / Nov 3, 1926

15204-D (as by Gid Tanner & His Skillet Lickers with Riley Puckett & Clayton McMichen)
....(Oct 31, 1927)
Old McDonald Had A Farm..................mx 145047-2
Big Ball In Town..............................mx 145049-1

15217-D (as by Gid Tanner & Fate Norris)
....(Nov 1, 1927)
Please Do Not Get Offended..................mx 145056-2
Everyday Will Be Sunday Bye And Bye......mx 145057-1

15221-D (as by Gid Tanner & His Skillet Lickers with Riley Puckett & Clayton McMichen)
Uncle Bud......................mx 145054-2 / Oct 31, 1927
Johnson's Old Gray Mule......mx 145058-2 / Nov 1, 1927

GID TANNER (& His SKILLET-LICKERS)

15237-D (as by Gid Tanner & His Skillet Lickers with Riley Puckett & Clayton McMichen)
Casey Jones....................mx 143785-2 / Mar 28, 1927
Buckin' Mule....................mx 145053-2 / Oct 31, 1927

Gid Tanner Cont.

15249-D (as by Gid Tanner & His Skillet Lickers with Riley Puckett & Clayton McMichen)
....(Oct 31, 1927)
Bile them Cabbage Down......................mx 145048-3
It's A Long Way To Tipperary..................mx 145050-3

15267-D (as by Gid Tanner & His Skillet Lickers with Riley Puckett & Clayton McMichen)
....(Apr 10, 1928)
Slow Buck...mx 146005-3
Sal Let Me Chaw Your Rosin...................mx 146007-2

15283-D (as by Gid Tanner & His Skillet Lickers with Riley Puckett & Clayton McMichen)
....(Apr 10, 1928)
Cotton Eyed Joe..................................mx 146002-2
Black Eyed Susie................................mx 146003-2

15298-D (as by Gid Tanner, Clayton McMichen, Riley Puckett, Lowe Stokes & Fate Norris)
....(Apr 13, 1928)
Possum Hunt On Stump House Mountain Part 1
....mx 146056-3
Possum Hunt On Stump House Mountain Part 2
....mx 146057-1

15303-D (as by Gid Tanner & His Skillet Lickers with Riley Puckett & Clayton McMichen)
....(Apr 10, 1928)
Hen Cackle..mx 146000-1
Cumberland Gap................................mx 146001-1

15315-D (as by Gid Tanner & His Skillet Lickers with Riley Puckett & Clayton McMichen)
....(Apr 10, 1928)
Prettiest Little Girl In The County.............mx 146004-3
Settin' In The Chimney Jamb...................mx 146006-1

GID TANNER (& His SKILLET-LICKERS)

15334-D (as by Gid Tanner & His Skillet Lickers with Riley Puckett & Clayton McMichen)
Liberty..........................mx 147253-1 / Oct 22, 1928
Pretty Little Widow............mx 147263-2 / Oct 23, 1928

15382-D (as by Gid Tanner & His Skillet Lickers with Riley Puckett & Clayton McMichen)
....(Oct 22, 1928)
Nancy Rollin.......................................mx 147254-2
Old Dan Tucker..................................mx 147255-1

15404-D (as by Gid Tanner & His Skillet Lickers with Riley Puckett & Clayton McMichen)
....(Apr 8, 1929)
Show Me The Way To Go Home..............mx 148209-1
Cotton Baggin'....................................mx 148210-2

15420-D (as by Gid Tanner & His Skillet Lickers with Riley Puckett & Clayton McMichen)
....(Apr 8, 1929)
Mississippi Sawyer.............................mx 148200-1
Going On Down Town.........................mx 148202-2

15447-D (as by Gid Tanner & His Skillet Lickers with Riley Puckett & Clayton McMichen)
....(Apr 8, 1929)
It Ain't Gonna Rain No Mo'...................mx 148201-2
The Rovin' Rambler............................mx 148211-2

15468-D (as by Gid Tanner, Clayton McMichen, Riley Puckett, Lowe Stokes & Fate Norris)
....(Apr 13, 1928)
Hog Killing Day Part 1.........................mx 146058-3
Hog Killing Day Part 2.........................mx 146059-2

15472-D (as by Gid Tanner & His Skillet Lickers with Riley Puckett & Clayton McMichen)
....(Apr 8, 1929)
Flatwoods...mx 148203-2
Never Seen The Like Since Gettin' Upstairs..mx 148208-1

15485-D (as by Gid Tanner & His Skillet Lickers with Riley Puckett & Clayton McMichen)
....(Oct 29, 1929)
Boneparte's Retreat............................mx 149280-2
Cripple Creek.....................................mx 149283-2

GID TANNER (& His SKILLET-LICKERS)

15516-D (as by Gid Tanner & His Skillet Lickers with Riley Puckett & Clayton McMichen)
....(Oct 29, 1929)
Rocky Pallet..mx 149276-2
Hell's Broke Loose In Georgia................mx 149281-2

15538-D (as by Gid Tanner & His Skillet Lickers with Riley Puckett & Clayton McMichen)
....(Oct 29, 1929)
Soldiers Joy..mx 149277-2
Rock That Cradle Lucy..........................mx 149278-1

15562-D (as by Gid Tanner & His Skillet Lickers with Riley Puckett & Clayton McMichen)
....(Apr 14, 1930)
Sal's Gone To The Cider Mill.................mx 150204-2
Nigger In The Woodpile.........................mx 150205-2

15589-D (as by Gid Tanner & His Skillet Lickers with Riley Puckett & Clayton McMichen)
....(Apr 15, 1930)
Devilish Mary......................................mx 150222-2
Soldier, Will You Marry Me....................mx 150223-2

15612-D (as by Gid Tanner & His Skillet Lickers with Riley Puckett & Clayton McMichen)
....(Apr 14, 1930)
Sugar In The Gourd..............................mx 150202-2
Georgia Wagner...................................mx 150203-2

15623-D (as by Gid Tanner & His Skillet Lickers with Riley Puckett & Clayton McMichen)
....(Apr 14, 1930)
Leather Breeches.................................mx 150200-2
New Arkansas Traveler..........................mx 150201-2

15640-D (as by Gid Tanner & His Skillet Lickers with Riley Puckett & Clayton McMichen)
....(Dec 5, 1930)
Bully Of The Town No.2........................mx 151042-2
Broken Down Gambler...........................mx 151043-2

GID TANNER (& His SKILLET-LICKERS)

15665-D (as by Gid Tanner & His Skillet Lickers with Riley Puckett & Clayton McMichen)
....(Dec 4, 1930)
Ride Old Buck to The Water....................mx 151024-1
Don't You Cry My Honey.......................mx 151025-2

15682-D (as by Gid Tanner & His Skillet Lickers with Riley Puckett & Clayton McMichen)
....(Dec 4, 1930)
Cacklin' Hen And Rooster Too.................mx 151026-2
Ricketts Hornpipe................................mx 151027-2

15695-D (as by Gid Tanner & His Skillet Lickers with Riley Puckett & Clayton McMichen)
....(Oct 29, 1929)
There'll Be A Hot Time In The Old Town Tonight
....mx 149279-1
Giddap Napoleon................................mx 149282-1

15709-D (as by Gid Tanner & His Skillet Lickers)
Devilish Mary...................mx 147256-2 / Oct 22, 1928
Fly Around My Pretty Little Miss
..................................mx 147264-2 / Oct 23, 1928

15716-D (as by Gid Tanner & His Skillet Lickers with Riley Puckett & Clayton McMichen)
....(Dec 6, 1930)
If You Want To Go A Courtin'.................mx 151061-2
You've Got To Stop Drinking Shine...........mx 151062-2

15730-D (as by Gid Tanner & His Skillet Lickers with Riley Puckett & Clayton McMichen)
....(Oct 24, 1931)
Miss McLeods Reel.............................mx 151916-1
Whistlin' Rufus..................................mx 151921-1

15746-D (as by Gid Tanner & His Skillet Lickers with Riley Puckett & Clayton McMichen)
....(Oct 24, 1931)
Four Cent Cotton................................mx 151917-1
Molly Put The Kettle On.......................mx 151918-1

GID TANNER (& His SKILLET-LICKERS)

15777-D (as by Gid Tanner & His Skillet Lickers with Riley Puckett & Clayton McMichen)
....(Oct 24, 1931)
Sleeping Lulu......................................mx 151919-1
McMichen's Breakdown........................mx 151920-1

JIMMIE TARLTON
15629-D...(Dec 3, 1930)
New Birmingham Jail...........................mx 151004-2
Roy Dixon..mx 151005-3

15651-D
Careless Love....................mx 151000-2 / Dec 3, 1930
Moonshine Blues................mx 151010-1 / Dec 4, 1930

15763-D..(Dec 3, 1930)
By The Old Oaken Bucket Louise............mx 151001-2
Lowe Bonnie......................................mx 151002-2
(See Tom Darby & Jimmie Tarlton)

ERNEST THOMPSON
15000-D...(Sept 11, 1924)
Alexander's Ragtime Band....................mx 140033-3
Mississippi Dippy Dip..........................mx 140034-2

15001-D...(Sept 9, 1924)
Sylvester Johnson Lee..........................mx 81987-2
Weeping Willow Tree..........................mx 81961-1

15002-D (as by Ernest Thompson & Connie Sides)
....(Sept 10, 1924)
Silly Billy..mx 81993-1
At A Georgia Camp Meeting.................mx 81992-1

15006-D...(Sept 11, 1924)
When You're All In, Down And Out.........mx 140001-1
Whistling Rufus.................................mx 140000-1

15007-D...(Sept 9, 1924)
I'm Going Down To Jordan....................mx 81985-2
Old Time Religion...............................mx 81984-3

GEORGE THOMPSON
(Pseudonym for Frank Luther *(see Carson Robison (15532-D)*

UNCLE JIMMY THOMPSON
15118-D..(Nov 1, 1926)
Billy Wilson......................................mx 143002-2
Karo...mx 143004-2

REV. M.L. THRASHER & His GOSPEL SINGERS
15207-D..(Nov 9, 1927)
What Shall We Do With Mother...............mx 145180-2
When The Roll Is Called Up Yonder..........mx 145182-1

15239-D..(Nov 9, 1927)
Wonderful Grace................................mx 145181-2
There's Glory On The Winning Side...........mx 145183-2

15271-D..(Apr 18, 1928)
When I See The Blood Of The Lamb..........mx 146130-2
Where The Soul Never Dies.....................mx 146131-2

15294-D..(Apr 18, 1928)
The Last Mile Of The Way......................mx 146132-2
You Shall Reap Just What You Sow..........mx 146133-1

15313-D..(Nov 9, 1927)
Ring Out The Message..........................mx 145178-2
At The Cross.....................................mx 145179-1

Rev. M.L. Thrasher Cont.
15335-D..(Oct 25, 1928)
I'll Keep Singing On............................mx 147287-2
Walk In The Light Of God.....................mx 147288-2

15361-D..(Oct 25, 1928)
Just As I Am....................................mx 147289-2
We'll Drop Our Anchor........................mx 147290-3

15396-D **(as by The Thrasher Family)**
....(Apr 15, 1929)
My Savior's Love................................mx 148299-1
Reapers, Be True................................mx 148300-2

15422-D..(Apr 15, 1929)
Just To Be Alone With Jesus...................mx 148288-2
Beautiful Home Awaits.........................mx 148289-2

REV. M.L. THRASHER & His GOSPEL SINGERS

15459-D..(Apr 15, 1929)
No Room...mx 148286-1
Jesus Knows How.................................mx 148287-2

15484-D..(Oct 28, 1929)
Don't Forget to Pray............................mx 149267-2
When We Go To Glory Land..................mx 149270-2

15539-D (as by The Thrasher Family)
....(Oct 28, 1929)
This Is The Reason..............................mx 149272-2
He Will Be With Me..............................mx 149274-2

15571-D..(Oct 28, 1929)
My Old Cottage Home..........................mx 149268-2
The Answer Comes Back......................mx 149269-2

15607-D..(Oct 28, 1929)
Redeemed...mx 149266-1
Standing On The Promises...................mx 149271-1

15717-D (as by The Thrasher Family)
....(Oct 28, 1929)
I Have A Friend...................................mx 149273-2
It Was For Me.....................................mx 149275-1

THREE GEORGIA CRACKERS
See Canova Family

BILL TUTTLE
15697-D..(Dec 10, 1929)
The Roamin' Musician..........................mx 149576-2
Gamblin' Bill Driv' On..........................mx 149577-2

CECIL VAUGHN
15465-D..(Sept 25, 1929)
Out In The Cold World And Far Away From Home
....mx 149047-1
The Village Blacksmith.........................mx 149048-2

BILLY VEST (The Strolling Yodler)
15602-D..(Sept 19, 1930)
Yodeling Hobo.....................................mx 150827-2
A message from Home.........................mx 150828-3

BILLY VEST (The Strolling Yodler)

15669-D...(Apr 16, 1930)
She'll Never Find Another Daddy Like Me
....mx 150239-2
I Loved You Better Than You Know..........mx 150240-2

15692-D...(Apr 17, 1931)
Billy's Blue Yodel.....................................mx 151521-2
She Died Like A Rose..............................mx 151522-2

GEORGE WADE & FRANCUM BRASWELL
15515-D...(Oct 21, 1929)
Think A Little..mx 149204-2
When We Go A Courtin'..........................mx 149205-2

GEORGE WALBURN'S FOOTSCORCHERS
15721-D...(Oct 30, 1931)
Halliawika March....................................mx 151990-1
Dixie Flyer..mx 151991-1

DOCK WALSH
15047-D...(Oct 3, 1925)
The East Bound Train..............................mx 141089-1
I'm Free At Last......................................mx 141098-1

15057-D...(Oct 3, 1925)
Bull Dog Down In Tennessee..................mx W141096-1
Educated Man..mx W141097-2

15075-D...Apr 17, 1926)
Knocking On The Hen House Door.........mx 142029-2
We Courted In The Rain..........................mx 142032-2

15094-D...(Apr 17, 1926)
Going Back To Jericho............................mx 142033-1
In The Pines..mx 142031-1

15105-D
Traveling Man..................mx 142028-2 / Apr 17, 1926
See Gid Tanner & Faith Norris 15105-D

A.E. WARD & His PLOW BOYS
15734-D...(Oct 25, 1931)
The Old Dinner Pail................................mx 151924-1
Going To Leave Old Arkansas................mx 151925-1

WARNER & JENKINS
See W.C. Childers

W.L. RUSTIC WATERS
15705-D...(Aug 24, 1931)
Lonely As I Can Be................................mx 151746-2
Sweet Nora Shannon............................mx 151747-2

WEAVER BROTHERS
15487-D...(Oct 22, 1929)
You Came Back to Me............................mx 149236-1
Prison Sorrows.....................................mx 149237-2

WEEMS STRING BAND
15300-D...(Dec 9, 1927)
Davy...mx 145355-2
Greenback Dollar..................................mx 145536-2

W. W. WEST (Rattler)
15013-D...(Jan 31, 1925)
Puttin' On Airs.....................................mx 140311-1
Sambo..mx 140312-2

WESTBROOK CONSERVATORY PLAYERS & SOLOIST
1574-D...(Nov 3, 1931)
The Old Rugged Cross............................mx 152025-1
I Would Walk With My Saviour.................mx 152026-?

WHEAT STREET FEMALE QUARTET
15021-D...(Jan 1925)
Wheel In A Wheel.................................mx 140200-1
Oh, Yes!..mx 140301-1

WILKINS QUARTET
15592-D...(Apr 18, 1930)
I Am So Glad.......................................mx 150279-2
Glory For The Faithful............................mx 150280-2

WILLIAMS & WILLIAMS
15172-D...(Mar 29, 1927)
In The Garden......................................mx 143803-2
Though Your Sins Be As Scarlet................mx 143804-2

FRANK WILSON & His BLUE RIDGE MOUNTAIN DUO

15372-D...(Feb 20, 1929)	
Polly Ann...mx 147971-1	
Katy-Did Waltz...................................mx 147975-1	

THE WISDOM SISTERS

15093D..(Apr 23, 1926)
Sitting At The Feet Of Jesus...................mx 142097-2
Amazing Grace...................................mx 142096-2

15112-D..(Nov 4, 1926)
A Charge To Keep................................mx 143053-1
Jesus Is All The World To Me..................mx 143054-2

15129-D..(Nov 4, 1926)
Children Of The Heavenly King................mx 143052-1
The Old Time Power.............................mx 143055-2

15153-D..(Mar 30, 1927)
Hide Thou Me.....................................mx 143817-2
Saviour More Than Life To Me.................mx 143818-1

15309-D..(Mar 30, 1927)
Prayer..mx 143819-2
Why Not Say Yes.................................mx 143820-2

EPRAIM WOODIE & The HENPECKED HUSBANDS

15564-D..(Oct 24, 1929)
The Last Gold Dollar.............................mx 149260-2
The Fatal Courtship..............................mx 149261-1

WRIGHT BROTHERS QUARTET

15402-D..(Apr 17, 1929)
God's Message To Man.........................mx 148326-2
What A Glad Day..................................mx 148327-2

15587-D..(Apr 17, 1929)
Mother Is With The Angels.....................mx 148328-2
Somebody's Boy..................................mx 148329-2

WYATT & BRANDON

15523-D..(Oct 21, 1929)
Evalina..mx 149214-2
Lover's Farewell..................................mx 149215-2

IRA & EUGENE YATES
15581-D
Powder And Paint……………..mx 149262-2 / Oct 23, 1929
Sarah Jane…………………...mx 149263-1 / Oct 24, 1929

JIMMY YATES
See Red Mountain Trio

JESS YOUNG
15219-D (as by Young Brothers Tennessee Band)
…………………………………………...(Nov 8, 1927)
Bill Bailey……………………………...mx 145166-2
Are You from Dixie…………………….mx 145167-2

15338-D (as by Jess Young's Tennessee Band)
…………………………………………..(Oct 25, 1928)
Fiddle Up……………………………...mx 147293-2
Oh! My Lawd…………………………..mx 147294-2

15400-D (as by Jess Young's Tennessee Band)
………………………………………….(Apr 19, 1929)
Sweet Bunch Of Daisies……………….mx 148361-2
Silver Bell……………………………...mx 148362-2

15431-D (as by Jess Young's Tennessee Band)
…………………………………………..(Apr 19, 1929)
The Old K-C…………………………...mx 148363-2
Lovin' Henry…………………………...mx 148364-2

15493-D (as by Jess Young's Tennessee Band)
…………………………………………...(Nov 4, 1929)
Take A Look At The Baby…………….mx 149348-2
Old Weary Blues………………………mx 149349-2

BIBLIOGRAPHY

The following reference sources were used for the valuable information provided in this guide.

The Almost Complete 78 RPM Dating Guide: by Steven C. Barr – Huntington Beach, CA, Published by Yesterday Once Again 1992

American Record Labels And Companies An Encyclopedie (1891 – 1943): by Allan Sutton & Kurt Nauck – Highlands Ranch, CO, Mainspring Press 2000

Country Music Records A Discography 1921 – 1942: by Tony Russell & Bob Pinson– New York, New York, Oxford University Press 2008

Virginia's Blues, Country & Gospel Records 1902 – 1943 An Anotated Discography: by Kip Lornell – University Press of Kentucky 1989

American Premium Record Guide 1900-1965 6th Edition: by Les Docks – Krause Publications, Books Americana, Iola, WI 2001

<u>Southern Historical Collection</u> at the Wilson Library University of North Carolina at Chapel Hill

<u>Southern Folklife Collection</u> at the Wilson Library University of North Carolina at Chapel Hill

BluegrassMessengers.Com

Folk Music Index (ibiblio.org)

American Folklife Center (Library of Congress)

Adair, Green B. pg 5
Akins Birmingham Boys pg 5
Alabama Sacred Harp Singers pg 5
Albertville Quartet pg 5
Alcoa Quartet pg 5
Allen Brothers pg 5
Arkansas Woodchopper pg 5
Ashley, Clarence pg 5 - 6
Atco Quartet pg 6
Autry, Gene (see Overton Hatfield) pg 35
Barton, Ben & his Orchestra pg 6
Banjo Joe pg 6
Bateman Sacred Quartet pg 6
Bentley Boys pg 6
Birkhead, L.O. & R.M. Lane pg 6
Black Brothers (see Carson Robison & Frank Luther) pg 68
Blalock & Yates pg 6,
Blevins, Fank & his Tar Heels Rattlers pg 6 - 7
Blue Ridge Highballers pg 6
Blue Ridge Mountain Singers pg 6 - 7
Blue Ridge Singers pg 7
Borg, Benny pg 7
Boswell, Leo (& Dewey) pg 8, (see Elzie Floyd) 30, (see Merritt Smith) pg 71
Bouchillon, Chris pg 8 - 9
Bowman, Charlie & his Brothers pg 9
Bowman Sisters pg 9 – 10
Bradshaw, Carl (see Remus Rich) pg 66
Braswell, Francum (see George Wade) pg 88
Breaux, Clemo (see Joseph F. Falcon) pg 29
Brock, Jessie (see Earl McCoy) pg 42
Brock & Dudley pg 10
Brook, Charles S. (& Charlie Turner) pg 10
Brookes, Bob pg 10
Brooks, Billy pg 10
Brooks, Charles pg 10
Brooks, Richard (see Reuben Puckett) pg 59

Brown, Bill (see Clayton McMichen) pg 44 - 45
Bryant, Slim (see Clayton McMichen (McMichen's Georgia Wildcats) pg 49
Buice Brothers pg 10
Burnett & Rutherford pg 10 - 11
Burns, Jewell (& Charlie D. Tillman) pg 11
Bush Family (Bush Brothers) pg 11 – 12
Butler, Wallace Hotel DeSota Orchestra pg 12
California Aeolians pg 12
Canova Family pg 12
Carolina Buddies pg 13
Carolina Night Hawks (see Vernon Dalhart) pg 22
Carolina Troubador (see Dewey Hayes) pg 36
Carter, Buster (& Preston Young) pg 13
Cartwright Brothers pg 13 - 14
Cash, Elry pg 14
Childers, W.C. pg 14
Chumbler Family pg 14
Clarke, Luther B. pg 14
Classic City Quartet pg 14
Columbia Band pg 15
Conner, Carl pg 15
Cook, Herb pg 15
Copeland, Leonard (see Roy Harvey) pg 35
Copperhill Male Quartet pg 15
Corley Family pg 15
Cowboy Tom's Roundup with Chief Shunatona, Doug McTague & Skookum pg 15
Crain, Edward L. pg 15
Craver, Al (Vernon Dalhart) pg 18 – 24
Cross & McCartt pg 15
Cross, Hugh pg 16, 17 (see also Clayton McMichen pg 45 - 47 (see Riley Puckett) pg 64
Crow, Phil (see Carson Robison) pg 68
Dalhart, Vernon pg 18 - 24
Dalhart Texas Panhandlers pg 19

Daniels – Deason Sacred Harp Singer's pg 24
Darby, Tom & Jimmie Tarlton pg 24 - 27 (see Jimmie Tarlton) pg 85
Davis, Claude pg 27
Davis, Claude Trio pg 27
Deal Family pg 27 - 28
Delmore Brothers pg 28
Denson Quartet pg 28
Dixie String Band pg 28
Dorsey, Tom (see Clayton McMichen) pg 46 - 49
Duncan Sisters pg 29
Dupree, Melvin (See Bill Shores) pg 70
East Texas Serenaders pg 29
Edgin's, George Corn Dodgers with Earl Wright & Brown Rich pg 29
Etowah Quartet pg 29
Evans, Clyde Band pg 29
Evans, Roy pg 35
Everhart, Clay & North Carolina Cooper Boys pg 29
Falcon, Joseph F. pg 30
Ferguson, Bob (see Bob Miller) pg 50 - 52
Ferguson, Bob & his Scalawaggers (see Bob Miller) pg 50 - 51
Floyd, Elzie (& Leo Boswell) pg 30
Ford, Oscar pg 30 – 31 (also see Clayton McMichen) pg 47 - 48
Foss, Joe & his Hungry Sand Lapper's pg 31
Freeman & Ashcraft pg 31
Ganus Brothers (Ganus Brothers Quartet) pg 31
Garland Brothers & Grinstead pg 31
Garner, Clem (see Earl McCoy) pg 42
Gates, Johnnie (The Saw Mill Yodeler) pg 31
Gatwood Square Dance Band pg 31
Georgia Organ Grinders pg 32
Godwin. Shorty pg 32
Gordon County Quartet pg 32
Gossett, Fred & Gertrude pg 32
Grady Family pg 32
Grant Brothers pg 32
Greene, Clarence pg 32 - 33
Greensboro Boys Quartet pg 33

Grisham, Mr. & Mrs. R.N. (& Daughter) pg 33
Hack, E.E. String Band pg 33
Hampton, Sid pg 34
Happy Four pg 34
Happy Jack pg 34
Hare, Ernest pg 34
Harold, Richard pg 34
Harris, George E. pg 34
Harper, Roy (see Earl Shirkey & Roy Harper) pg 35
Harvey, Roy (North Carolina Ramblers) pg 35 (also see Earl Shirkey & Roy Harper) pg 69 - 70 (see Charlie Poole) pg 59
Hatfield, Overton pg 35
Hawkins, Miner pg 35
Hawkins, Ted Mountaineers pg 36
Hayes, Dewey pg 13
Helms, Bill (with Riley Puckett) pg 65
Helton, Ed Singers pg 36
Hendersonville Double Quartet pg 36
Higgins, Len & Joe pg 36
Hodgin, Willard (See Banjo Joe) pg 6
Home Town Boys pg 36
Hood, Adelyne (see Vernon Dalhart) pg 22 - 23
Hornsby, Dan (Trio, Novelty Quartet, Novelty Orchestra, Lion's Den Trio) pg 36 - 37 (see also Clayton McMichen) pg 44
Jackson, Jack pg 37
Jackson. Molly Aunt pg 37
Johnson, James pg 37
Jones, Colon (with Riley Puckett) pg 65
Jones, Roy pg 38
Jones, Sam (See Stovepipe #1) pg 76
Kentucky Girls pg 38
La Dieu, Pierre pg 38
Layne, Bert (see Georgia Organ Grinders) pg 32 (see Clayton McMichen) pg 43, 47 - 49 (see McMichen-Layne String Orchestra) pg 45 - 46
Leake County Revelers pg 38 - 40
Legette, Malcolm pg 40
Lubbock Texas Quartet pg 40
Lunsford, Bascom pg 40

Luther, Frank (See Carson Robison) Pg 67 - 68
Mack, Dick (see Bert Swor) pg 76
Macon Quartet pg 40
Mahoney, Jack pg 40
Major, Jack pg 41
Malone, K.D. (see Clayton McMichen) pg 45
Marlor, John (see Marshall Smith) pg 71
Martin Melody Boys pg 41
Marvin, Frankie pg 41
Marvin, Johnny pg 41
Marvin Family (see Frankie Marvin) pg 41
Massanutten Military Academy Quartet pg 41
Mathis, Jack pg 41
McCartt, Luther (see Hugh Cross) pg 15
McCartt Brothers & Patterson pg 41
McConnell, Ed & Grace pg 42
McCoy, Earl (& Jessie Brock,) (Alfred Meng, Clem Garner) pg 42
McCoy, William pg 42
McCravy, Frank & James pg 42
McGimsey, Bob (See Bob Brookes) pg 10
McMichen, Clayton pg 43-49 (also see Georgia Organ Grinders) pg 32 (see Riley Puckett) pg 65 (see Gid Tanner) pg 79 - 85
McMichen's Georgia Wildcats with (Slim Bryant) (see Clayton McMichen) pg 49
MicMichen-Layne String Orchestra (see Clayton McMichen) pg 45 -46
McMichen's Melody Men (see Clayton McMichen) pg 43 - 47
McMillan Quartet pg 49
McTague, Doug & Skookum (see Cowboy Tom's Roundup) pg 15
McVay & Johnson pg 49
Melton & Waggoner pg 49
Memphis Bob (see Bob Miller) pg 19

Meng, Alfred (see Earl McCoy) pg 42
Miller, Bob pg 50 - 52
Miller, Charlotte (see Bob Miller) pg 50

Moatsville String Ticklers pg 52
Montgomery, Rev. C.D. pg 52
Moore, Byrd & his Hot Shots pg 52
Morris, Walter pg 52
Mount Vernon Quartet pg 52
Murphy Brothers Harp Band pg 53
Myers, Hinky pg 53
Nichols, Bob (See Clayton McMichen) pg 43-49 (also see Claude Davis) pg 27
Norris, Faith (Fate Norris) (see Gid Tanner) pg 79
Norris, Fate (& his Tanner Boys, & his Play Boys) Pg 53 (see also Georgia Organ Grinders) pg 32 (see Clayton McMichen) pg 43 - 48 (see Gid Tanner) pg 80 - 82
North Canton Quartet pg 53
North Carolina Cooper Boys (see Clay Everhart) pg 29
North Carolina Ramblers led by Posey Rorer (see Charlie Poole) pg 56 – 57 (see Roy Harvey) pg 35
North Carolina Ridge Runners pg 53
Owens, E.B. pg 53
Owens Brothers (& Ellis) pg 53 - 54
Paramount Quartet pg 54
Parker, Charlie & Mack Woolbright pg 54 - 55
Parker, Chubby & his Old Time Banjo pg 55
Parker, Peggy pg 55
Pelican Wildcats pg 55
Penny, Old Hank pg 55
Pickard, Obed of Station WSM, Nashville, TN pg 55
Pickell, Jack pg 55 - 56
Poole, Charlie (with the North Carolina Ramblers) pg 56 – 60 (North Carolina Ramblers led by Posey Rorer) pg 56 - 57 (& Roy Harvey) pg 59
Praetorian Quartet pg 59
Proximity String Quartet pg 59
Puckett, Reuben pg 59

Puckett, Riley pg 60 - 65 (see also Hugh Cross) pg 16 - 17, (see Clayton McMichen) 43 - 49 (see Lowe Stokes) pg 76 (see Arthur Tanner & his Corn Shuckers) pg 29 (see Gid Tanner) pg 78 - 85
Rainey Old Time Band pg 65
Rann, Grover & Harry Ayers pg 66
Rector Trio pg 66
Red Mountain Trio pg 66
Reed, Bill & Belle pg 66
Reed Children pg 266
Rich, Brown (see George Edgin's Corn dodgers) pg 29
Rich, Remus & Carl Bradshaw pg 66
Richards, Fred pg 66
Roane County Ramblers pg 67
Roark, George pg 67
Robison, Carson & Frank Luther pg 22 (Travelin' Jim Smith) pg 25., (& Phil Crow) pg 68 (as Black Brothers) pg 68 (& His Pioneers) pg 68
Roe Brothers & Morrell pg 68
Rogers, Ernest pg 69
Roper's Mountain Singers pg 69
Rorer, Posey (see Roy Harvey) pg 35 (see Charlie Poole) pg 56 - 60
Royal Sumner Quartet pg 69
Saw Mill Yodler (see Johnnie Gates) pg 31
Sawyer Sisters pg 69
Shamrock String Band pg 69
Shelby Singers (See Bob Miller) Pg 51
Shell Creek Quartet pg 69
Shirkey, Earl (& Roy Harper) pg 69 70
Shores, Bill & Melvin Dupree pg 70
Shunatona, Chief (see Cowboy Tom's Roundup) pg 15
Sides, Connie pg 71 (see Ernest Thompson) pg 85
Sims, Oliver pg 26
Skidmore, Bud (See Bob Miller) pg 51
Smith, Charles B. pg 71
Smith, J. Frank (See Smith's Sacred Singers) pg 72
Smith, Travelin' Jim (see Carson Robison & Frank Luther) pg 67

Smith, Marshall & John Marlor pg 71
Smith, Merritt & Leo Boswell pg 71
Smith's Sacred Singers pg 71 - 74
Snowball & Sunshine pg 74 - 75
Snowball, Rev. (see Snowball & Sunshine) pg 75
Spindale Quartet pg 75
Spooney Five pg 75
Stanley, Fred pg 75
Stamps Quartet (see Owens Brothers & Ellis) pg 54
Stapleton Brothers pg 75
Stephens, Uncle Bunt pg 75
Stine, Charles Lewis pg 75
Stokes, Lowe (& His North Georgians, With Mike Whitten) pg 76 (also see Georgia Organ Grinders) pg 32 (see Clayton McMichen) pg 44 - 49 (see Gid Tanner) pg 81 - 82
Stovepipe #1 pg 76
Stringfellow Quartet pg 76
Stroup Quartet pg 76
Sunshine Four pg 76
Swor, Bert & Dick Mack pg 76
Tanner, Arthur (& his Corn Shuckers) pg 77 - 78
Tanner, Gid (& his Skillet Lickers) pg 78-85 (also see Clayton McMichen) pg 43 - 49 (& Faith Norris) pg 29 (Gid Tanner's Georgia Boys) pg 78
Tarlton, Jimmie pg 85 (also See Tom Darby & Jimmie Tarlton) pg 24 – 27
Texas Cowboy, The (see Edward L. Crain) pg 15
Thompson, Ernest (& Connie Sides) pg 85 (see Connie Sides) pg 71
George Thompson (See Carson Robison & Frank Luther) pg 67
Thompson, Uncle Jimmy pg 86
Thrasher, Rev. M.L. & his Gospel Singers pg 86 - 87
Thrasher Family pg 86
Three Georgia Crackers (See Canova Family) pg 12
Tillman, Charlie D. (see Jewell Burns) pg 2

Tuttle, Bill pg 87
Uncle Bud & his Plow Boys (see Bob Miller) pg 51
Uncle Fuzz (see Clayton McMichen) pg 47
Vaughn, Cecil pg 87
Vest, Billy pg 87 - 88
Wade, George & Francum Braswell pg 88
Walburn's, George Footscorchers pg 88
Walsh, Dock pg 88
Ward, A.E. & his Plow Boys pg 88
Warner & Jenkins (See W.C. Childers) pg 14
Waters, W.L. Rustic pg 89
Weaver Brothers pg 89
Weems String Band pg 89

Wells, Charlie (see Vernon Dalhart) pg 20 - 22
West, W.W. (Rattler) pg 89
Westbrook Conservatory Players & Soloist pg 89
Wheat Street Female Quartet pg 89
Whitten, Mike (see Lowe Stokes) pg 76
Wilkins Quartet pg 89
Williams & Williams pg 89
Wilson, Frank & his Blue Ridge Mountain Duo pg 90
Wisdom Sisters pg 90
Wise Brothers (see Clarence Greene) pg 33
Woodie, Epraim & his Henpecked Husbands pg 90
Wright, Earl (see George Edgin's Corn dodgers) pg 29
Wright Brothers Quartet pg 90
Wyatt & Brandon pg 90
Yates, Ira & Eugene pg 34 (also See Blalock & Yates) pg 6
Yates, Jimmy (see Red Mountain Trio) pg 66
Young, Jess pg 91
Preston Young (see Buster Carter & Preston Young) pg 13
Young Brother's Tennessee Band (see Jess Young) pg 91

Young's, Jess Tennessee Band (see Jess Young) pg 91

CPSIA information can be obtained
at www.ICGtesting.com
Printed in the USA
FFOW03n1338050516
23877FF